Ulster Folk Stories for Children

ULSTER FOLK STORIES

for

CHILDREN

Paddy Tunney

THE MERCIER PRESS

The Mercier Press, 4 Bridge Street, Cork
24 Lower Abbey Street, Dublin 1

ISBN   0   85342 930 8

Typeset in Palatino by Seton Music Graphics Ltd, Bantry.

Dedication

*To Mary F. McGrath, my first teacher — who encouraged
me to write from an early age*

Printed by Litho Press Co., Midleton, Co. Cork.

Contents

1

The Story of Johnie Hump

The people of the mountain streams country will tell you to this day that Johnie McGee was born and grew up as straight as a yard of pumped water. He was a trim, trig,* thrifty little man who lavished care and affection on the snug house he lived in on the hip o' Rusheen hill.

He lime-washed it every spring and renewed the oat-straw thatch every five years. 'The sight of yellow thatch over white walls makes my heart lep!' he declared to his cousin Dan the Thatcher as that craftsman drove the last scollop home on the front of the roof in under the skew.*

His farm was small; eight acres of green land wrenched and retained from the hungry heather that fought hard to take over again. Still it was big enough to grow the potatoes and oats to keep the house going and the lint or flax to make the linen for the shirts and shifts of the household.

Along with green land Johnie had ten sums* on a common mountain where he was able to graze thirty to forty Scotch ewes and a ram so it was not surprising that he could be seen more times carrying the shepherd's crook than herdsman's ashplant.

From the half-door of Johnie's kitchen you could see three lakes, Lough a Leamhnacht, Lough Suimhneach and Rusheen Lough. All three lapped the fringes of Johnie's holding so that it was said that Johnie McGee had an endless supply of heather for life and water for eternity. His two black cows and their off-spring did not need to be driven to the water. They went on their own.

But Johnie had other irons in the fire. He was game-keeper and water-keeper in that district for the landlord and agents of the Leslie Estate and woe betide the poacher, heather puller or billberry picker he caught near the lakes or in the demense where the longest, besom-making heather and billberry bushes grew.

Indeed he seized the makings of a heather besom from my own mother, God rest her, and scutched* her round the legs with a long, black-sally rod when he met her on the road coming home from school.

Hens, ducks and geese thrived all round the McGee homestead for the hilly ground was dry and the hens could wallow in the mounds of turf mould and the ducks and geese with their chassis slung near to the ground had their choice of water to swim, wade and whuttle* in. So Johnie McGee and old Peggie, his widowed mother, had plenty of eggs to eat and sell in Pettigo market every Monday morning. Peggie had a spinning-wheel and spun woollen yarn for socks, stockings, shawls, and ganseys of every shade. She gathered the mosses and lichens off rocks and tree trunks to dye the wool. Her wheel was specially adjusted to spin lint into linen thread and, since lint could not be knitted, it was brought to the weaver two townlands away.

Johnie and Peggie were as near self-sufficienct as could be. They had only to buy the grain of tea and sugar and an odd pack of flour. Wee Mickie Trickie, the shoemaker up at Cruckadey, made their boots and shoes.

They lived in health and contentment until the day Johnie tangled with the travelling-man Bob Davitt. This is how it happened.

Bob was a knight of the road, odd in his manner, but always civil as long as no one put to him or from him. It was whispered that he was away to be a priest but the learning turned his head. Because of this he could not be priested and when he came out of college he took to roaming the roads and reading books about magic and the mysterious powers of nature. He peddled in safety-pins, whangs, the name for leather laces for strong boots, Rosary beads, holy pictures and sometimes swopped these articles for worn-out horse shoes, out of which he assured the hillmen he would make a bell.

He was staying this night in Mick Hugh's at the other end of Rusheen and Maryanne, the woman of the house, had some stomach ailment at the time.

'If only I could have a trout!' she wished, 'it is the one kind of food to give me back my appetite.'

Bob Davitt heard her remark and hastened to the lough shore where he set a night-line. Next morning he had his fine pound trout wriggling on the end of an eel-hook. He brought it up and it was cooking nicely on the tongs over hot coals when Johnie McGee crossed the threshold.

The water-keeper was on the hearth in three strides and reached for the fish.

'Who has been poaching?' he enquired in the tone of a bullying upstart.

'No one,' the man of learning told him gruffly, 'the good Lord who made all feathered and finned creatures intended them for all the people, not just a few.'

'I'm seizing this trout,' Johnie growled. 'I may have to summons you Mister Davitt.'

Bob Davitt was a big man. He grabbed Johnie by the back of the neck and held him out at arm's length.

'Will I throw him out to the ducks Hugh?' he asked derisively.

The fish fell out of Johnie's hand and the big tom cat bounded off the half-loft, snatched the trout and was over the half-door with it while you'd be saying Willie the Wisp. One word borrowed another. Before Bob could curb his anger he had cursed Johnie McGee not only with his left hand but also with his left foot.

No one likes to be cursed with the left hand. But to be cursed with the left foot is a frightful thing. Once the act is performed there is no escaping the consequences. Johnie had heard tell of the travelling-man's curse. He was truly shaken and left Mick Hugh's a very worried man.

Harvest time came and he had a bumper crop of corn. He sheared and stooked the corn and gathered it into stacks in his neat haggard. When threshing time came he brought half a stack into the kitchen and went out to fetch an outhouse door, that lifted easily off the hinges, to use as a threshing board. He had no time to thresh by day but would begin the work at night-fall in the light of an oil lamp.

He put the door in place and then went off for his flail. It should be hanging on the harness peg in the barn he told himself but when he went there it was not to be seen. He struck a match and surveyed the floor. He found the handstaff and supple right enough but they were uncoupled and the eel-skin tug that tied them together was eaten through by mice. That was it. He'd have to delay threshing for a week and set a line in the lough near Tullyvogie to catch an eel. Then it would take three or four days hanging on the crane-crook before the eel-skin would be seasoned enough to make a good tug.

He caught an eel all right the first night he set the line but it was such a reptile of an eel that he had to use the fir hatchet to cut the head off it. The eel was still wriggling when he hit him and as he cut clean through, the head gave a loud whistle and rolled away back down the heather and into the lake. The incident put the heart crossways in him but his bother was only starting.

In three days time the skin had dried out and he was able to convert it into a flail tug. He started threshing. All went well the first night, but when he woke in the morning the supple and handstaff lay side by side on the kitchen floor and the tug was gone.

He went out to fodder the cows and calves and there was a big bull calf lying on the stand, dead as a dodo. It had been strangled with the eel-skin tug! The travelling–man's curse — Johnie thought bitterly as he dragged out the calf and buried it. Should he bury a sheaf of corn along with it and bring death on Bob Davitt? But then it might boomerang upon himself! 'I'll let the hare sit,' he decided.

He seized the tug, took it in to the house and threw it in the fire. It became a live eel, complete with head, went wriggling up the chimney and he never saw it again. He made a tug of tow from the scutched flax and continued to thresh and never let on to old Peggie that the calf had been throttled.

On Halloween he headed for Breen Mountain to gather up his ewes. Mist blew up from the curragh and white-holes at the back of John Arrigles and very quickly he was astray. Now white-holes are pools of clear water in swampy moorland where bog-bean and muineogs* grow but if you went into them they'd swallow you up like quicksand. The word curragh is used to describe that kind of moorland. Willie the Wisp is often seen flitting about over these quagmires on dark winter nights and if you walked on the peaty ground near one of them the soles of your boots would be studded with glow-worms. Mist gathers quickly over such places and then swirls up to higher ground.

Johnie McGee was frightened out of his wits. Great drifts of fog shut out the dying daylight and the evening star. He had stumbled on to the fairy pass! Would he ever see Rusheen again? Then his faithful sheep dog gave a fright-ened yelp and sped off into the night. Dogs are quick to detect the presence of spirits and things that go bump in the night but will do almost anything to shun their company.

It was not Johnie's first time to go astray. He made the Sign of the Cross, took off his coat and put it on again inside out. Almost at once he saw a rock he recognised for the sheep had sheltered under it for years and made use of it for a scratching post. He went towards it. He could scarcely believe his eyes. There was a door in the rock and it was ajar! He went over and pushed it open.

Inside he found a long, narrow corridor with a light shining at the far end of it. He was drawn to the light as a moth is to a candle. When he came level with it he found it was a splint of bog-fir that blazed in an iron bracket which was driven into the rock. He moved on to find his way lighted by another bog-fir torch and yet another until he had penetrated a couple of miles into the hillside.

Suddenly he saw a heavy oak door completely blocking the passage. He walked up and tested it. It was not locked. The pleasant odour of cooking assailed his nostrils and for the first time since he left home he was hungry. Just then the door swung open and a pleasant voice called out: 'Welcome Johnie McGee, welcome to the Fort of the Shee!'

He entered a long, rectangular room well lighted with torches and at the far end sat the king and queen of the fairies on high thrones of beaten gold. In no time at all they had Johnie sitting up in the place of honour quite near to the royalty enjoying the feasting and the fun of that great banquet. As soon as he emptied his flagon it was refilled with the most wonderful liquor he ever tasted. Johnie thought that it must be mead. There were also lashings of roast pheasant, tender veal, rare venison not to speak of the grilled salmon and delicious brown trout.

There were other rare, aromatic dishes, served with the rich sauces and spices from the east and Johnie reckoned they must have come from the Garden of Eden and remained in cold storage since the Fall of Adam. He devoured them all and washed the food down with the beautiful drink he thought was mead.

In spite of all the food and drink, the rich variety and unending quantity, Johnie could not take his eyes off the fairy queen. She was a female of dazzling beauty and it seemed to him that if he did avert his eyes off her for a second her magnetism drew them back again to be greeted by the most adorable smile.

'Could it be that she has a grá* for me!' he thought but did not dare to voice this idea lest it would be judged to be high treason. But she continued to hold his gaze.

As Johnie raised his goblet to toast the king and queen and for one brief moment took his eyes off the object of his desire, he happened to glimpse twenty hairy hunchbacks perched high on harrow-pins that protruded from the walls on either side. Their faces were distorted in the most hideous grins and their general bearing was one of evil. A shudder ran down his spine and he got the feeling there was someone walking on his grave.

The feasting was followed by song and dance and the sweetest music that ever soothed the ear of a mortal. Then Johnie was asked to sing and since it was the fairy queen made the request he could not demur.

'What will it be your Majesty?' Johnie asked as he stood up and bowed very low.

'Surely you shouldn't have to ask. *The Mountain Streams Where the Moorcocks Crow*,' she told him. 'It's the song of the place for twice one hundred years. Mary Gallagher used to sing it beautifully. I once invited her to come here to the court and sing at a banquet but she refused. Not long after she died. What a sin such a voice couldn't live for ever. Had she come here I could have arranged that too.'

Johnie began to sweat but then the fairy queen cast upon him such an adorable smile that he was lost in her radiance. He then cleared his throat and sang that lovely song. The applause was thunderous.

Then it was time to put round the snuff. Although Johnie was completely lost in the beauty of the queen he distinctly heard the warning not to invoke the Almighty if a sneeze escaped a snuffer. A good habit is as hard to break as a bad one so when Johnie took his sniff and sneezed loudly his invocation to God for a blessing could be heard all over the banquet hall.

'Johnie McGee,' the fairy king roared, now livid with rage, 'you have abused the hospitality of your host. There is only one penalty and that is death for such a transgression!'

But the fairy queen, who had taken a fancy to Johnie, pleaded for clemency. The king was adamant. She beseeched him through floods of tears to show mercy.

'Very well,' he thundered, 'since I cannot stand a woman whinging, the sentence will be commuted. But he must be punished. Soldiers, take down those hunchbacks off the harrow-pins and put the twenty humps off them on to the broad back of Johnie McGee.'

And it was done.

There was sudden darkness. The walls of the fairy court fell away and Johnie found himself out in the swirling mists of the mountainside with the slua sí or fairy hosts.

'Bring me my steed,' shouted the fairy king and at once a prancing charger appeared and he rode away into the night.

'Bring me my horse,' called the fairy queen in words that were like music in Johnie's ears, and as quickly she was mounted and rode away after him.

'Give me a horse,' shouted each warrior in turn and immediately mounted and galloped off.

'Give me a horse,' Johnie made bold to ask and a fine snorting stallion stood before him. He sprang to the saddle and joined the slua sí in their headlong gallop over the bogs and plains of Ireland. Johnie soon came up to the royal couple for he had a fine, galloping steed and he reined in on the right of the fairy queen. The king raised no objections.

When it cleared daylight in the morning Johnie McGee found himself straddle-legged on a whin bush at the back of his own house, his rump punctured like a pin-cushion with sharp whin spikes.

He thanked God for delivering him from the fairy hosts but feeling the weight on his back, he put round his hand. It was too true! The horrible hump was there, weary and woeful as the heap of sin that weighs down the world.

2
The Wheeling Hare

They let Reynard go, that cunning old fox
That ate all their chickens, fat hens and game cocks
But I never was given to rob or to stale (steal)
Just in times of hard weather I'd crop the green kale

With my ochon tie ho! my terry hi ho!
I ne'er will recover, my terry hi ho!

'I learned that song from a hare,' Mickie Flanagan told us,
'I met one frosty evening on the headland of the turnip
field. Pull in your stools and forms to the hearth and
throw a couple of beech logs on the fire Charlie to keep
her bright and blazing. That's the good cub! And now let
us get on with our story,' and Mickie whisked us away to
the land of legend.

'Where was I? Oh, aye, Helen the Hare of course. She
was a very old hare you know who had seen more suns
sink and moons rise into the roof of the sky than any man
or beast before or since. Boys, oh boys don't I pity you
cubs who can't talk with your furred and feathered friends
at all!

'I'm sure you're all peppering to find out how I could
chat with her. It's really very simple you see; a gift given
to an odd man once in a life-time maybe. Very few could
get that gift today.

'In olden times before screeching trains and hooting
motor-cars got so plentiful we had horses and mules,
jennits, ponies and asses to carry or draw us round the
country. Sure they're as rare today as red snow or white
blackbirds! I had a tidy* little mare of my own and she

15

was due to have her first foal at the latter-end of April and I had to watch her like a fox.

'She held out until May Eve when the neighbours' children were gathering marsh marigold flowers to guard the people and their cattle against the spells of witches and boyos with the evil eye.* Some of them spotted her away in the far field near the heather — standing with her backside in the wind but making no attempt to graze. Ha, ha! thinks I, she's away to foal — and if she happens to drop her foal away out there in the field the witches use to milk the tether* every May Day dawn my foal could be turned into a toad or some other horrible quacking, squalling, misbegotten thing.

'You know how the witches milked the tether* in the old times?' he asked.

'We don't!' all of us chorused. 'You tell us.'

'At first light on May Day,' he began, 'the forces of evil are most potent. That's why Cormac MacArt, the famed Irish high-king, returned to the ramparts of Tara to make sure no evil spirits descended upon his kingdom from the upper air. A high-king had powers to defeat the spells and schemes of all wicked spirits and things of course.

'It is also the time witches descend off their broomsticks in a meadow at the centre of a townland and begin sweeping the dew into a ring they make with their brooms. As they sweep they keep up the chant: "come all to me! come all to me!"

'In this way they steal the butter off every churning in that townland and it matters not a whit how long your mothers work away at their crocks of cream in their churns they wouldn't be able to get as much butter off their churnings as would grease the gudgel of one turf-barrow! Not only that but the witches would have all the butter off their churnings for the entire year. Isn't it a sight boys!'

'A holy sight surely!' we agreed with one voice, but

were pretty shaken for Mickie Flanagan was never known to tell a lie. He smacked his lips and continued.

'I think boys you'll agree my unborn foal was in great jeopardy and so long before the sun winked an eye at the world that May Day I was up and away to mount guard over my livestock.

'I found the mare on the bruach* of the sheugh* in the far field licking the foal she had just dropped. It was then I cursed myself for a fool. Hadn't the foal the talisman to protect them both from all evil in this world and the next!

'I waited until the foal rose on rickety legs and staggered towards its mother for the first suck. Then I scrutinised the ground where it had lain. Sure enough there was the precious trefoil* growing rank and dark green on the spot where he had been dropped. I bent down and almost reverently plucked my four-leafed shamrock that springs forth only on the spot where a maiden mare drops her first foal.

'Now I had a tried and true protection from wicked spells, baleful blighters with the evil eye* and tether-milking witches. But I was given another gift too: that was to be able to understand and speak the language of the birds and beasts! Boys, oh boys! that was the greatest year I ever had chatting up all shapes and sizes of beasts and birds and lending an ear to the tales of weal and woe they told me.

'Funny thing though, Helen the Hare was the only one who ever taught me a song. Wouldn't you think now that the thrushes and blackbirds with all their traditions of music and song would have offered to teach me one of their tunes itself and they knowing I played the fiddle and all?

'Helen was a very proud lady and when she was young and agile never ceased searching for her roots. She remembered when she was at a hare university somewhere in the orchard country of Armagh hearing a venerable

hare historian holding forth on their species. He held that
hares were once a high and haughty race who had eight
legs instead of four. Why they had eight legs and were
eventually reduced to four was a constant source of wonder
and puzzlement to Helen. She set out to find the reason.

'First, she approached a great bull frog that lived at the
bottom of a spring well for longer than any living creature
could remember.

'"How would I know?"croaked the frog who had had a
'flu for forty years and had forgotten to gargle his throat
that morning. "I'm only five hundred years on earth. It
must have been before my time. Go to the Salmon of
Asseroe. He's twice my age and exceedingly wise. He'll be
apt to know."

'Away went Helen and never made land-dwelling nor
sea-stoppage until she arrived in Ballyshanny and the
island of Inish Samer. She asked a sea-trout juking* the
sunbeams on the southern bank of the Erne to slip over to
the great salmon and whisper in his ear that a fair maiden
was in distress and in dire need of help.

'The mighty fish was having a shower bath in the froth
of the Falls but sent her word he'd be over in a tick.* He
was as good as his word. Presently his royal highness
cruised towards her and she couldn't help admiring the
bulk and beauty of his body. He reminded her of a steep-
pitched stable roof slated with half-crowns.

'"O Salmon of Asseroe!" she began but he cut her short.

'"Cad chuige nach bhfuil tú ag caint i nGaeilge?" he
rebuked her. "Aodh Rua Ó Domhaill agus Aodh Rua Mac
Barronn, ní raibh Béarla ar bith acu."

'"Tá mo chuid Gaeilge caillte agam,"poor Helen told
him.

'"B'éigin domh tréimhse fada a chaitheadh imeasc na
nGall. An bhfuil cead agam a dul ar aghaigh i mBéarla?"
she begged.

'"Tá cead agat cinnte," he told her, "ach bí gearr."

'Then she put the question about the eight-legged hares.

'"Hares," said the salmon, with a husky haughtiness peculiar to sea-kings, "I never put much weight on them. They have no scales. They haven't even a decent tail!" Here he swished his immense rudder to underline what he meant. "No, I never heard of the hares with eight legs although I once heard a Kildoney fisherman, whose net I left in tatters, refer to you as lepers of ditches and clippers of thorns, just wee brown cows with pairs of leather horns. Not very complimentary I'm afraid," and the salmon laughed his husky, salt-sea laugh.

'Helen hated him with every hair of her fur coat but what good did that do her?

'"Of course I'm young in the world. One thousand years ago I was spawned in the Scardan River under Red Lawns. I was only a grilse at the time of the Battle of Clontarf. We were nearly choked in the blood of Vikings that year and we swimming past Beann Eidear! Go west to Prehan Acla or the Crow of Achill. He's twice my age. I once heard him boast he was a scaldie* the day the sun darkened and a god was slain somewhere in the Middle East. . ."

'Helen headed on. She ran very fast through the small neck of Leitrim that separates Donegal from Sligo for she had heard tell of the Leitrim folk and how they stole Saint Patrick's goat because he levelled their idols on Maigh Sleachta or the Plain of Adoration. They chased him as far as the River Drowes and might have done the holy saint an injury were it not for the good-natured shoal of salmon that formed up to make a bridge for him to cross into sainted Donegal. Indeed it was whispered he hadn't a great deal of time for Leitrim folk for he maintained that the wives there had sharper tongues than their husbands' swords! Would you believe that boys?

'High on the slopes of Ben Bulben she spent that night on a rocky flag once slept on by Dermot and Gráinne when they ran away from the wrath of Finn MacCool. She dreamt that night of giant hares with eight legs running round Ireland and hiding in the hills from the famous hounds of the Fianna.

'At dusk on the third day she reached Achill far out on the coast of the County Mayo. The Crow of Achill had been picking the bones of a mighty ram that had fallen to his doom over one of the cliffs near Duagh and he was full. He needed the night to sleep off the effects he said and asked Helen to call back next morning.

'So our bullaí* hare retired to the security of the Corran or Reaping Hook where she gorged herself with a tightener* of lettuce and then crept deep into the heather to sleep the sleep of the just.

'Next day she returned to the cliffs of Achill where the Prechan or Crow was awaiting her.

'"Hares. . ." cawed the famous Crow in a strong Mayo accent, "are lovely animals . . . to eat. They're sweet and wholesome but I never heard tell of a hare with eight legs!

'"In the Irish they call you giorria or little hares. I suppose up in Ulster they'd call you wee deers. Maybe you were big deers with eight legs once upon a time but that must have been before I sprouted wings. After all I'm only a mere two thousand years flying around but I'm told before that there used to be mighty scenes and sights.

'"Go to the Cailleach Bearra or the Hag of Beara. She's twice my age and still skipping about like a two-year-old. She's sure to have seen the eight legged hares if the like were ever in it."

'Poor Helen! She was distressed and distraught. Still she kept right on and followed her nose. She made the cliffs of Moher that night and picking a spot far out on the crags where even the most daring dog wouldn't venture, she made a den in a sweet-scented clump of herbs and slept as if she were back on the slopes of Slieve Gullion, her native heath.

'Three more days racing and pacing brought her

through Bantry to the bothóg* or hut of the Hag of Beara. The Cailleach was hunched up on a creepy stool raking the red gríosach* of a burnt out fire for a bit of heat. Helen the Hare introduced herself politely and mentioned her errand.

'"Ho! ho!" croaked the Hag in a hoarse, crackling voice; "hare soup, hare soup! where would the Hags of Ireland be without it!"

'A shiver went down Helen's spine but she did not panic.

'"The ru, the su," went on the Hag, "the knuckles of a bumbee! No earthly good at all! I'd as leif* be drinking whey. But hare soup. Give me hare soup every time! It's meat and kitchen to a Cailleach!

'"I may as well admit I'm the oldest creature alive I've seen the pomp and power of kings: the glory and grandeur of emperors. Where are they today? Tumbled down and beaten into the dust. Daughter dear I was in Troytown with Hector. I was the friend of kings. And now I'm the lonely Hag of Beara waiting for God to summon me. I, the princess who courted Cuchulann and bound up his battle scars!"

'Helen's heart went out to the renowned Cailleach and she lost all fear of her.

'"Of course I remember your mighty ancestors, the hares with eight legs. They were much larger than you. 'Tis said Noah had two of them in the Ark the time of the forty–day shower.

'"They ran on all fours till they tired and then switched to the back fours; I mean the ones sprouted out of their backs. The Celts came and bred large hounds to catch them. So well did they succeed that at one time they were nearly extinct.

'"Then a very clever forefather of yours thought of a ploy to best even the wolfhounds. Let the hares become hoops and hurl away from the hounds by rotating their bodies on all eight legs in a wheel-like motion! It worked. No hound that was ever bred could match the speed of the wheeling hare. How could he catch it?

'"One day a craftsman was watching one of these hares hurling away like a Will O' the Wisp over the horizon. The idea struck him: why not a spoked wheel to replace the heavy, solid one?

'"Immediately he went into his workshop and built the first spoked wheel and joined the spokes together with naves. A blacksmith forged an iron hoop to keep the naves in place.

'"And that's how you hares gave the world the spoked wheel that became the hub of science and locomotion!"

'"I have reason to be proud then?" ventured Helen, suffused with a glow of satisfaction that her quest had not been in vain.

'"You have not," screeched the Hag. "Pride comes before a fall. That's exactly what befell your eight-legged ancestors. They became puffed up with pride. God punished them as he did Lucifer. Their back legs disappeared and eventually they were reduced to the sawn-off creatures you are to this very day. All he left you was that spirit of nobility that keeps you going to the last gasp when being hunted down. So Helen dear, no airs or graces!"

'Helen hadn't the heart to go back to Slieve Gullion instead she stayed with me for the remainder of her days.'

'What about the four-leafed shamrock?' Charlie asked. 'Will you leave it to me when you're going to die?'

Mickie fell away back in the big armchair and he shook with laughter.

'Trust a McGuare to make such a request!' he commented. 'Still they say you're very fond of birds and beasts so I suppose you'll have to be forgiven this time. Truth is it's no longer mine for the giving. I kept that shamrock safely in my waistcoat pocket until the summer Helen the Hare died. The cows were late a-calving and I went to the fair of Ballintra and bought a cow to keep us in milk.

'That old crubach* was never right for she ate towels, tea-cloths and any article of clothing she got around the hedges and ditches. There came a very fine spell of weather that summer and the heat was powerful. This day I was moulding potatoes in the moss and the sweat was lashing off me. I clean forgot about the four-leafed shamrock and took off my waistcoat. I left it lying on the road at the head of the broken ground and when I got the call for dinner forgot to bring it with me.

'When the crubach* got me out of sight didn't she lep the barb-wire fence that guarded the laboured land and devour waistcoat and the contents of its pockets!

'We should have slaughtered her and retrieved the talisman out of her stomach but then you wouldn't like to do that and besides there was no guarantee that she would not have the shamrock digested.

'For years after that you'd think it a sin to see beasts and birds lining up for the bit of crack and the divil a word Mickie could say to them. Without the four-leafed shamrock I clean forget their language you see. Boys o' dear, wasn't it a terror?'

Poor Mickie, he never found another four-leafed shamrock nor neither did we.

3

The Magic Spade

Tom Flannery was a giant of a man. He stood six feet six inches in his stocking soles, had a back broader than a barn door and arms that went down below his knees. Still, it was the hands you noticed first. When he gripped a full-size football in one of them it seemed no bigger than a sliotar.* He was feared by most men, especially by those who stood shoulder to shoulder with him on a football pitch but loved by all women. Fine well they knew that such men were getting as rare as golden eagles.

He togged out for his club and county as full-back and no forward ever scored a goal against his team when Tom defended the square. Instead they shot from thirty yards out, and they were lucky to notch the odd point. So it was not surprising that big Tom was often flown home to play games in the west after he joined the garda síochána and found himself posted to Dublin. On many occasions he was known to arrest and bring to the station three of the toughest characters to be found in the inner city if he saw them brawling. He usually took one in each hand and one in his mouth. If the fellow swinging from his jaws gave an unruly wriggle at all Tom threw him into the air with a little jerk of the head and caught him in his teeth coming down. Small wonder that the crime rate fell steeply when Tom was stationed in Dublin.

He loved fishing and fowling and never tired of singing 'one morning as I went afowling' or that other great traditional favourite that begins: 'with my dog and gun through the blooming heather, to seek for pastime I took my way.' His voice would not exactly coax the birds off the trees but he could have reached up and grabbed the

24

birds if he so wished. Sure you can't have all the natural gifts.

However, wild-geese do not alight or nest in trees but must be sought where you're likely to find them and so Tom went in quest of them with his dog and a neighbour's gun.

One Christmas when he was home on holidays and the other young heroes were away hunting the wren on Saint Stephen's Day, Tom borrowed a double-barrelled gun and headed away to a lonely mountain lough where he had made a goose-hole during the dry summer season. Now a goose-hole is dug out of the peaty bank of a lough and lined with dry heather when the weather is fine. Hence it is that a fowler can go out there in colder times and wait in the goose-hole, comfortable and well camouflaged, until the geese arrive from the Artic to their winter quarters. If he's lucky he'll get at least one shot in before they take flight to some other remote lough or swampy wet land.

He lay in the goose-hole for nearly three hours but not a single goose came next or near the lough. He climbed out and made for home, hungry as a hawk and in a very bad mood. Not as much as a feather to show for his long vigil! He'd be the laughing stock of the four townlands. And the footballers wanted him to play in that good fellowship game against Charlestown!

A freezing fog blew up from the marshes and soon furred the hills and hollows over which he hurried. Then, as he neared home, he heard the honk of wild-geese. He crept into a clump of whins and waited. They were still hidden in the fog but by the direction the honking came from they seemed to be heading for the little lough at the bottom of Martin Merrick's meadow. Suddenly they swooped down through the mist, semi-circled and settled down on the water. He was in a perfect position. They were within range though the light was fading fast. He could wait no longer.

He put the fowling-piece to his shoulder and pulled left and then right. It was then he heard the unmerciful yell and as he jumped out of hiding was in time to see old Martin keel over by the potato pit. 'Mother of God!' he exclaimed, 'I have shot him', and cold sweat broke out all over him. He was sick at heart and cursed the geese.

Then he panicked. Throwing the gun from him he ran all the way to the cross-roads pub and ordered a bottle of whiskey. Until that evening he never knew the taste of liquor and had faithfully kept his Confirmation pledge. He had gulped down three glasses of the fiery water and was beginning to feel a little fuzzy when the door flew open and in burst old Martin Merrick, the man Tom thought he had shot.

'Oh, glory be to God!' the old man gasped, 'there's a miracle after happening. I was hoisting a sack of potatoes on to my back above at the potato pit when four geese dropped down out of the mist and lighted on the lough. I threw down the sack and from force of habit, put the spade to my shoulder, taking aim between the lugs. "If only you were a gun," I wished. With that didn't the spade go off with two unmerciful bangs and it must have been the kick of her that stretched me on the broad of my back by the mouth of the pit. When I came to again I could just make out in the gathering dusk the shape of four white things down in the bullreeds. I went to see and there were my four dandy wild-geese floating in the water as dead as dodos. Did you ever hear the likes of it?'

Tom was so glad he had not shot the old codger and that he would not be arrested, sentenced and hanged by the neck until he was dead, that he seized old Martin in his arms, carried him over to the big pub fire and brought him a glass of brandy. He kept his secret until Martin died for he thought it would be a sin to tell the truth and wreck a lovely legend.

The fame of the magic spade spread away out over the

plains and hills of Mayo and into Coleman country round Riverstown and Ballymote. Pious and superstitious men came to see the weapon and marvel at the potency of its power. Martin showed it proudly to all of them but was most careful never to point it at anyone.

'You see, one has to be careful with spades,' he warned them. 'They don't have safety catches.'

4
Blacksallymare

'Blacksallymare! That's a strange name for a townland?' I put the question to Ned Noble as he stood on the steps of my wooden caravan-dwelling in the county council road depot above in Donagh.

'And the story of its naming is just as strange,' he gave me back, but none the less it true.'

He was on his way home from harvesting with the MacIllgunns and was parched with thirst he declared. Remembering another MacIllgunn and the Bunnan Buí or Yellow Bittern he found on the frozen waters of either Loughmacnean or Lough Erne I was anxious that Ned wouldn't suffer the same fate.

'What about a mug of buttermilk?' I suggested.

'Prime,' he exclaimed, 'prime. In fact the very thing the doctor ordered. All them leeches I met when I was over in Manchester getting the cancer cut off my lip maintained it is the best food or drink ever entered a man's stomach! And it slides down your gullet like suds down a sink!'

I brought him the buttermilk, he drank it with relish that confirmed the faith he had in doctors' opinions. Then he smacked his lips and handed me back the empty mug.

'Come on away in,' I invited him. 'Davy, my roller-man's gone to Clones. He won't be back till bed-time.'

'No, I won't g'win this evening. Some other evening when the hay's saved and the lint's pulled maybe I'll ceilí* with you. When a man comes to my time of day he gets very stiff after a heavy seige of work forking meadow hay. When he sits down it gets hard to rise again.

'But where was I? Oh, aye, Blacksallymare.

'There was a man lived in these parts one time they

28

called Sammie Wilson. He was a carrier by trade and drew all the liquor that landed at Lisnaskea railway station from breweries and distilleries in Bushmills, Belfast aye and even Dublin, to the publicans and inn-keepers of the town. His mode of conveyance was a long, low, four-wheeled dray, drawn by one of the finest specimens of blood-stock seen in Ulster since the prancing steeds that drew Cuchulann's chariot.

'She was a grand, high-stepping bay mare, seventeen hands high with a hide as silky as a seal and a head she threw back in real thorough-bred style. Indeed she was too noble to be yoked to a dray and only showed her paces between the shafts of a trap when Sammie travelled to far-off places such as Easnadarragh and Magheraveely to attend cock-fights or poteen sprees. It was then a sight to gladden your heart to see her flash between the hedges of narrow sandstone roads, knocking splanks out of the hard road metal with her well-shod hoofs.

'Came the Twelfth of July and Sammie did not know whether to turn up at the Orange Fleadh Cheoil or continue to draw liquor to the town hostelries so that no tongue would die at the root for want of proper liquid. In the heel of the hunt he settled for a day of honest toil and so his dray trundled between the railway station and the town until the sundial pointed due north and the Angelus bell rang out loud and clear.

'Then he unyoked the mare and hitched her to a rail in the yard at the rear of McCarroll's public house. The heat was so strong that it threatened to explode in a thunder storm and his tongue was thick in his head with drooth.* Furtively he stole into the pub by the back door to have a quick one before he opened his lunch bag.

'It was not his lucky day. The place was swarming with friends and neighbours and all of them wanted to treat Sammie. In the clapping of your hands his cares were forgotten and he was standing on the counter leading in the singing of "The Sash" and many other old traditional songs. In the hub-bub and babble of voices he forgot his mare standing lonely and forlorn out in the yard.

'Man dear, but it was a hot day! The crows were putting out their tongues and the heat was splitting the stones. There was a big barrell of porter primed up on a step at the back door in readiness to be tapped. With the shocking heat that was in it the gas pressure built up and the bung blew. The mare rose on her hind legs with fright, the throat strap of the winkers broke and there she was as free as the swallows that swished and swittered round the yard. Her thirst was great. She crossed to the stream of porter flowing down the yard and she drank her fill and a little more. Until that fateful day she didn't know the taste of intoxicating liquor. She liked it and drank away until she collapsed in an ungraceful heap of horse-flesh on the cobble-stones of the yard.

'To say that she was out for the count would be putting it mildly. When Sammie came back there wasn't a gig or a geg in her. The horse-doctor was brought. He was a travelling horse-doctor, highly skilled in the wiles and ways of horses and if a horse went lame in a leg he promptly lamed her in the other one so that a prospective buyer wouldn't notice the limping defect.

'"Dead as a dodo!" was his pronouncement and that was that.

'"Sammie, " he went on, "we'd better skin her at once. Yerrah, with the terrible heat and the blue-bottles it will be no time till she starts to smell!"

'Sammie's heart bled but what could he do? So they fell to with a big barber's knife and a shoe-maker's gullie they borrowed off a local cobbler and had the job finished just as the Orange bands began to pass in the parade. The boom of the Lambegs, the din of Kettle-drums and the skirl* of war-pipes, shook and rattled the windows of the houses and scattered the crows and the gulls in ragged flocks of flurried confusion away back as far as the Knocks.

'With all the rí-rá and ruaille-buaille* didn't the mare come to, for she wasn't dead but in a state of suspended animation, leaps to her feet and away round the yard like the hammers of hell. The horsey men, one and all, were scared out of their wits for although they had heard tell of a ghostly coach with four black horses drawing it, they had never met the ghost of a skinless mare before.

'Sammie rubbed his eyes. Was he seeing right? Stories of men's visions when in a state of intoxication referred mostly to elephants or maybe great, writhing serpents but skinless mares!

'It was the horse doctor who first realised that it was no ghost they had on their hands but a very live, skinless mare. They'd be the laughing stock of the country if word of what happened got out. They'd have to act. There was no time to lose. He found a bucket of oats in the stable and lured the mare to the food. By degrees they got the winkers on her again, hobbled her and gurgled a bottle of brandy down her gullet to act as an anaesthetic and then eased her down on a blanket spread over a sprinkling of sand at the bottom of the yard. Very, very carefully they scolloped the skin back on the mare with blacksally scollops they cut from the hedge outside of McCarroll's garden. It was a slow and tedious task.

'Sammie, who was a good thatcher and always thatched his own dwelling-house and out-offices, reckoned that he'd have no bother extracting the rods when the punctures they made had healed. After all the stitches were easily taken out after surgery.

'But the sally rods did not wither but grew profusely, sending out strong tenacious branches. Sammie was distraught. He could never harness his mare again! Still, he would not agree to her being put down but let her graze on his farm as long as breath was in her bones.

There was no hope of uprooting the blacksally bushes. The animal would bleed to death. So he groomed her as best he could and cut enough bundles of scollops off the branches she sprouted to thatch every house in the townland.

'As the mare got older the clump of sally bushes wore her thin and her head was deafened with the twitter of small birds coming to rest in the sally branches. She cursed the day she tasted porter, lay down in the meadow field and died. She had waited a life-time for the great stallion of a waterhorse that dwelt deep down in Lough Erne to come ashore on the night of a full moon and lure her away to a Tir-na-nÓg below the waves but the baleful blacksallys had blighted her life.

'Sammie wept bitterly and resolved never to take another drop of intoxicating liquor. He buried the noble beast where she fell at the head of the meadow but there was no need to raise a stone. The blacksallys sprung up in abundance on the spot where she lies and spread out to form a veritable wood.

'The powers that be at that time, in their wisdom and generosity, agreed to the changing of the name of the townland where Sammie lived to Blacksallymare. And so it has remained to honour the memory of a wonderful mare and as a warning to all men who worship at the shrine of Bacchus.'

5
The Grain of Oats

In olden times when pigs were swine and turkeys smoked tobacco and swallows made their nests in old men's beards and homes were thatched with pancakes, there lived a celebrated piper by the name of Horatio Alexander Cogadh Clancy.

Now this Horatio Alexander preached a doctrine alien to Ireland at the time that work, or honest toil as the lazy landlords called it, was the curse of God and should be shunned if at all possible and not only did he preach this gospel but he practised it religiously. Horatio slept all day and piped all night so that the great set-dancers came from all over the country to step it out to his music. There was no talk of payment. Hadn't he his board and lodging and lashings and lashings of food and drink wherever he chose to roam and the whole country was his home including a strip of the Kingdom of Kerry on the banks of the Shannon.

Not only did Horatio excel on the pipes, he could wield a camán* with the best too. Still it was as a stick fighter he was famed and feared. It is stated on good authority that he cracked more skulls of landlord's agents at fairs and gatherings of that sort than any other ash-plant wielder in Ireland at the time. No wonder that the epithet cogadh* was added to his many-handled name for he was indeed a mighty warrior.

Finally he was arrested and taken to court for beating up a big bodach* of a bailiff who had been bullying the small-holders at that time. His lawyer was the Liberator Dan O'Connell himself and Horatio got off with a suspended sentence. However, he was forbidden to carry an ash-plant in public places for ten years.

Then our warrior piper fell in love and settled down to married life. Still, he never betrayed his principles and continued to shun the curse of God.

But the pancake thatch began to be replaced with slates and tiles with the result that Horatio had to look elsewhere for food. He started music classes and soon was surrounded by a host of eager pipering men but the fees for his tuition were hard to collect and when one of his two cows died with the crupán* he was compelled to take the other one to the fair to get money to pay the rent.

The cow had calved late and Horatio had never weaned it and so he let the calf run along to the fair with its mother lest she and it would fret if he separated them.

He was standing on the fair green for three hours and no cattle-dealer had asked him where he was going when up stepped the bailiff whose skull he had tested with his ash-plant.

'How much are you asking for the little cow along with the calf over there by the gate?' the bodach* asked Horatio.

The piper was so taken by surprise that the bailiff would think of offering him a bid that he never dreamt it was a loaded question.

'£8,' he replied and waited for the buyer's next move.

'I'll give you the £8 but there will have to be a crown back,' the bailiff told him.

'Agreed,' Horatio said for he felt his cow was well sold.

The bailiff pulled out a purse of gold sovereigns and counted out eight of them which he handed to the piper.

'You needn't bother putting them down to Murphy's yard. I'll be heading home with them in a minute.'

'Them? I don't understand!'

'You don't,' the bailiff scoffed him. 'I bought the calf too. I said the cow along with the calf.'

'You're a cheat along with being a bailiff!' roared Horatio.'I thought you meant the cow alongside of the calf!'

'You did, did you?' the other sneered. 'I said the cow along with the calf! You can be sure O'Connell won't get you out of this hole.'

What could Horatio do? He had to grin and bear it. The calf was worth at least another £3. He was now left with the calf of the crupany cow* that died. It was the only four-footed beast on his small-holding if one excluded the cat.

But the Liberator got him a cushy little job for a year in his own country near Derrynane. He'd have to teach thirty or forty young Kerrymen the warpipes. The Liberator was teaching them English and so fortified with words and music they could join the English army and help to keep down the Ulster Presbyterians and such rebellious factions who sought to upset the benign reign of an English monarch in Ireland. Horatio was slow to train the Kerrymen but the rent had to be paid and the Battering Ram* was busy at the time all over the country.

So when his year was up he returned home to his wife and child and found the crupany cow's calf grown to a fine, thriving stirk.* He bought a springing cow off a neighbour and headed for the fair with the stirk.* The immortal Dan had let him into a secret and he was well prepared for the bailiff.

He hadn't long to wait. Up the green came the odious character swinging a big cudgel of a stick. He approached Horatio.

'How much do you want for the little stirk* Horatio?' he enquired in his overbearing, bullying manner.

'I'm not asking cash,' the piper told him, 'only the worth of the doubling of a grain of oats for half-an-hour.'

'The doubling of a grain of oats for half-an-hour! The man's mad.'

'The worth of the doubling of a grain of oats for half-an-hour,' Horatio corrected him.

'Fair enough but isn't it the same thing?'

'There was a conflict of meaning in our last deal. I wish it to be known that you and all these good men around us understand what the terms of the deal are.'

'He's mad. Completely mad!' one of his next-door neighbours commented. 'Either the Kerry air has moidered* him or he's afraid of the bailiff.'

All nodded their heads gravely in agreement.

Two members of the RIC with batons bigger than their feet, joined the knot of men surrounding the bailiff and Horatio.

'You've heard the terms. Please see that both buyer and seller adhere to them.'

'Japers!' exclaimed one of the peelers, 'O'Connell must have been teaching him English too. Repeat the terms piper,' he commanded and glowered at Horatio comptemptuously.

'The calf is on offer to this gentleman for the worth of the doubling of a grain of oats for half-an-hour. Is that clear?'

'I agree to your terms,' the bailiff shouted good-humouredly for he honestly thought Horatio had taken leave of his senses.

'Constable, will you consent to be time-keeper?' the bailiff asked.

'Of course I will,' that loyal limb of the law assured him, and took out a large, silver pocket watch, ''Tis now three o'clock. Begin, piper.'

'Right!' said Horatio and licked his lips:

'A grain and a grain is two grains.
Four grains.
Eight grains.
Sixteen grains.
Thirty-two grains.
That's a head.

A head and a head are two heads.
Four heads.
Eight heads.
Sixteen heads.
Thirty-two heads.
That's a handful.

A handful and a handful are two handfuls.
Four handfuls.
Eight handfuls.
Sixteen handfuls.
Thirty-two handfuls.
That's a sheaf.

A sheaf and a sheaf are two sheaves.
Four sheaves.
Eight sheaves.
Sixteen sheaves.
Thirty-two sheaves.
That's a stook.

A stook and a stook are two stooks.
Four stooks.
Eight stooks.
Sixteen stooks.
Thirty-two stooks.
That's a stack.

A stack and a stack are two stacks.
Four stacks.
Eight stacks.
Sixteen stacks.
Thirty-two stacks.
That's a haggard.

A haggard and a haggard are two haggards.
Four haggards.
Eight haggards.
Sixteen haggards.
Thirty-two haggards.
That's a townland.

A townland and a townland are two townlands.
Four townlands.
Eight townlands.
Sixteen townlands.
Thirty-two townlands.
That's a parish.

A parish and a parish are two parishes.
Four parishes.
Eight parishes.
Sixteen parishes.
Thirty-two parishes.
That's a barony.

A barony and a barony are two baronies.
Four baronies.
Eight baronies.
Sixteen baronies.
Thirty-two baronies.
That's a county.

A county and a county are two counties.
Four counties.
Eight counties.
Sixteen counties.
Thirty-two counties.
That's all Ireland and a country.

A country and a country are two countries.
Four countries.
Eight countries.
Sixteen countries.
Thirty-two countries.
That's a continent.

A continent and a continent are two continents.
Four continents . . . '

'Oh, for God's sake stop!' cried the bailiff, 'you have me ruined!'

'And you're only doubling for five minutes!' chuckled the constable whose whole attitude had changed for he greatly admired the craftiness of the piper.

'All right!' whined the bailiff. 'I know when I'm beaten. No need to rub it in. Come down to the bank. Will you settle for a thousand sovereigns?'

'Guineas!' asserted the piper. 'And it's not next or near the value of the oats I have piled up. You're getting a great bargain.'

'All right! I suppose there's little else I can do. My hand's in the dog's mouth. But you'll have to give me a good luck penny back. At least £50!'

'I won't be bound, I won't be bound!' shouted the piper now in his element, 'but I'll treat you decent.'

Both men headed off for the bank and Horatio the Piper never knew a hungry day from that day out. The people took courage from their piper; courage that helped them to endure the ravages of the Famine and the cruelties of absentee landlords.

To this day they can dance away their worries and their pipers, fiddlers and concertina players can set toes a-tapping even when the summer is not a sunny one and the hay that should be won is still in grass-cocks.

6

The King of Tullagh's Son

There is a long, low ridge of ground on the Milford side of
Carrigart in County Donegal and in old times when the
world was young it had its own king. Now wasn't it a
strange thing that a place so small and remote could have
a king of its own but, stranger things have happened
before and since.

The king had only one son and he christened him
Ceadach and he was known far and wide as Ceadach, son
of the King of Tullagh. When he grew up his father
couldn't hold him on any ground for he was smitten with
'itchy feet'. This meant that he wanted to be travelling and
seeing for himself what was happening in other places.
His father advised him to tarry a little longer because he
was young and the world was wide but nothing would do
him but get away.

At length the King gave him his head and Ceadach
went away to search for his fortune. Going out where
Kilmacrennan is today whom should he meet but the
mighty Finn MacCool who was making potín the same
day over near the Doon Well. He bade Finn the time of
day and they fell to chatting. Finn was as saucy as a Ballyshannon woman on a Harvest Fair Day so he enquired off
Ceadach what was his name and where was he going.

'Man sir,' says Ceadach, 'I'm off to search for my
fortune and find a wife — some one like the Greek King's
daughter or Helen of Troy!'

'Hold on now,' says Finn, cute as a jailor, 'one thing at a
time. I'll give you good money if you hire with me. The
horses have to be looked after, the stables dunged out and
those two hounds of mine need their toe-nails pared and

hardened or else they won't be able to take down the great elk any more. How much are you asking for a year and a day?'

'Oh, that depends,' says Ceadach. 'If you don't like me or my work I won't take a penny but if I satisfy you we'll talk about cash or kind when my time's up.'

'Fair enough,' says Finn. 'The bargain's clinched.'

Time passed and on the evening of the last day Finn went to Ceadach. 'I never hired a better hand in my life,' says he. 'How much will you be wanting?'

'A stout ship provisioned for seven years,' Ceadach told him.

'Granted!' says Finn for he was never a man to beat about the bush. 'She'll be ready for you in the morning,' and she was. Ceadach went on board and hoisted the mainsail that ceaped* every breeze and breath of wind wafted up off the broad bosom of the ocean. He heard the bellowing of great bull seals, the blowing of massive white whales and the splash of silver salmon through spray. Life and love coursed through his veins as he tramped the deck and felt the salty tang of the sea on his lips.

And where did he land? At the front of the court and castle of the Viking King! There was a thick wood of spruce growing down almost to the sea-shore so that he was able to moor the ship to a tree trunk and slip through the wood to the castle unnoticed. He hung around the castle for days and slept in the stables by night and no one put to him or from him. They took him for one of themselves as he had a good working knowledge of the Norse language learned in the course of a couple of days.

This day he was stravaiging* about in the woods when he spied a big, ugly gazebo of a building that was frightening and unfriendly to behold. Its top feather was in and its tail feather out and one great feather sheltered and shaded the lot of them. Away in goes Ceadach and it happened to be a schoolhouse. All the pupils were wee grawls* of children squealing and whinging in a large class for low infants with the exception of one big boy.

The boy came over to Ceadach and asked him who he was and where he had come from. Ceadach told him he was son of the King of Tullagh away back in the bowels of Donegal, 'but,' says he, 'who have I the honour to be addressing?'

'Oh, sorry. I should have introduced myself. I'm Felim, son of the Viking King. This is our kingdom.'

'Well, that beats fighting cocks!' says my bold Ceadach. 'We're both princes then?'

'You could say that I suppose,' says Felim, 'but princes today are a penny a dozen. Now if a man was a king itself he'd have something to crow about.'

'Hold your tongue,' Ceadach advised him, 'you must crawl before you walk.'

'No Viking ever crawls. He is taught to fight and kill but never to crawl, not even when he's an infant. Let us cut the cackle. Come on away in now. I'm sure my father will be pleased to meet you.'

The Viking King was lying over the half-door of the castle chewing a mouthful of uncut tobacco. His teeth were stained brown with it and the juice was streaming down his whiskers.

'Felimeen fair, where did you find this big highwayman?' he enquired.

'Father dear, he's no highwayman. That's Ceadach, son of the King of Tullagh out of Donegal in Ireland.'

The King advanced and held out an immense Viking paw.

'Put it there if it was a ton weight! You're as welcome as the flowers of May. Sure I know Donegal like the back of my hand! Many's a ship-load of scrap gold and silver I bought from Balor Beimeann, the king of Tory island when he was alive and well. Wasn't Luagh Laimh Fada his grandson, the divil to slay him, up at the top of the

Poisoned Glen? Man dear yon was a wild eye he had. I was always scared stiff when we'd be making a deal that he'd manage to lift the eye-lash and wither me like a dock, after frost, with one blink from it! Had he a big funeral?'

'In soul he had! They brought him back to Tory and waked him for seven days and seven nights and he "bled" better than any Kerryman whoever kicked the bucket. There were lashings and leavings of potín, wine and brandy, and they say a couple of jars of mead even. Then they burned his body on a great funeral pyre and they were boating turf from Bloodyforeland for days to make the fire.'

'Do you tell me so!' says the Viking King, 'and what did they do with his ashes?'

'Scattered them on the waves of the western ocean. The waves howled in protest and blew up a mighty storm that nearly swept away Tory island altogether.'

'My O!' sighed the Viking King. 'Neptune and Balor never got on well together. But what are we standing here for? Come on away in till you get a bite to eat. Sure you must be perished with the hunger! You'll stay a year and a day with us anyhow.'

Ceadach sat in to the table with the King and Felim and he ate a good tightener.*

'Now Felim would you ever rustle up a couple of polar bear skins for Ceadach. I'm afraid the blankets are light ones on our spare bed.'

When the time had expired and Ceadach was perfectly fluent in the Norse language his feet got itchy again. He wanted to go further afield and learn Greek. In those days the language of the outland races was all right, but the people had for regard on you at all if you couldn't discourse in the tongue of Homer.

He confided in Felim.

'I'll go with you,' says Felim. 'I want to learn Greek too.'

'I'll tell you what,' says Ceadach, 'it would be a cruel

thing if I were to take you from your parents and your heritage after the friendliness and hospitality shown to me here.'

But it was all to no purpose. Felim maintained that if Ceadach wouldn't take him on board he'd rig his own ship and head for the isles of Greece on his own. Ceadach knew he was a bad navigator. Once or twice when they had gone fishing and hunting Felim had put the whole party ar seachrán* with his clumsiness and lack of leadership.

'All right,' says he in a state of exasperation, 'be ready to sail with us in the morning.'

They went aboard and with a fair wind and fine weather it was no time at all until they arrived in Greece.

This time there was no woods growing down to the shore so they tied the ship to a stake and headed inland. The first building they saw was an ugly one in a state of disrepair. They went in and found it to be a schoolhouse. Most of the pupils were infant class children just like those back in Norse country but there was one big girl amongst them and she was the most beautiful creature either of them ever had seen.

In they went and Ceadach sat down beside the princess. If he did itself Felim was not to be denied for he sat down on the other side of her.

When three o'clock came and the pupils were dismissed all went out. The Greek King's daughter spoke to them and asked them who they were and did they come far.

'I'm Ceadach, son of the King of Tullagh beyond in Ireland,' says Ceadach, 'and my friend is son of the Viking King from Norseland. If you don't believe us you can take us captive. But with respect, would you tell us who you are?'

'Ah,' says she, 'that's no great mystery. I'm Anna, the Greek King's daughter.'

They told her they came to learn Greek so without any more ado she brought them in to her father.

The King was delighted to see them and made them more than welcome.

'Look boys!' says he, 'that's a very damp, draughty old school you were in today and the teacher's getting old and forgetful. I'll give you a new school and Anna will be your teacher.'

All went well from that day until the day they left. Ceadach was a very good student and not only did he learn the language much faster than Felim but he also studied Greek literature and philosophy and was able to spout Homer and Aristotle all over the place.

A year and a day passes quickly especially when you're being taught by a beautiful princess so when their time was up Ceadach announced that he'd have to depart next morning.

Felim was in a quandary. He didn't want to go and he couldn't possibly stay since the King's term of hospitality had expired.

It was then he confided in Ceadach that he was madly in love with the Greek King's daughter.

'Hold your tongue man!' Ceadach bade him, 'I'm out of my mind about her too, but since you were first to speak you must get the first chance. I'll tell you what. There're two doors on the school, the very grand one in front with the level walk leading to the road and a rough side door leading straight up cliffs and ivy-clad boulders. When we are leaving you go out by the front door and I'll go out by the side door. Who ever the princess follows is the one who will take her as his wife.'

'Fair enough,' says Felim, 'we'll shake hands on that.' And they did. When the time came Ceadach went out the side door and headed away through the rocks and boulders. Felim left by the front door and when he looked round there was no one to be seen, but when Ceadach looked round there was the Greek King's daughter climbing the rocks after him. By the time Felim got round to the gable of the school he saw Ceadach bounding up the rocks and the Greek King's daughter straggle-legged on his shoulders. He gave chase and shouted on his friend to halt.

'I'd halt surely Felim,' Ceadach hollered back, 'only I fear you would take the princess from me if I did.'

'I won't take her from you,' says Felim, 'if you grant me one request.'

'I'll grant you any request but the one asking for the surrender of the princess to you.'

'My request is that you grant me the striking of the first blow when we come face to face again,' says Felim.

'I grant you that,' says Ceadach and he and the Greek King's daughter headed away for the ship, singing of the Sack of Troy in Homeric couplets. In a short time they reached Ireland and went as far as Finn MacCool's camp.

Finn was beside himself with joy to see Ceadach again and fixed up decent living quarters for them for he wouldn't let them apply for a county council dwelling. 'That would be a shocking come-down for you altogether,' he declared.

He and Finn went hunting every day and sure it was like old times. They were away hunting this day and when they returned the Greek King's daughter was nowhere to be seen. She had been kidnapped. What was worse they didn't know whether it was down to the Underworld or up to the Upperworld they had taken her.

Ceadach had a hunch that it was down they headed with her so away he goes like the hammers of hell down to the Lower or Underworld. He was not too long below when he saw a great gathering of people near a schoolhouse and he approached them. He was in his Sunday best and very well dressed. All the nobility of the Underworld were present and they had just put the Greek King's daughter to death. They never dreamt the Ceadach was her husband.

He kept his cool and enquired why they had killed the princess. 'Oh, did you not know?' one of them asked him, 'we have tried these ten years to capture her and put her to death but it was only today we got an opportunity. You see, the Greek King can only be killed with a sword that has been honed on the blood of his daughter — we had to kill her in order to slay him.'

The sword was there sharp and keen and still dripping with the blood of Anna, Ceadach's beloved wife.

Then they started passing the sword around from warrior to warrior to make sure that all were of the opinion it was sharp enough. At length it was put in the hands of Ceadach, for they took him to be one of their own. As soon as he got it he beheaded the man nearest to him and as the other fighting men were not carrying arms he cut the heads off every man present — it was a bloody sight I can tell you. Heads rolling here and trunks lying there and blood flowing and dripping everywhere.

Then he went into the school and found his wife lying dead and the head cut off her. He put her body over his right shoulder and the head under his oxter* and he made no long pause or stoppage until he arrived at the court and castle of the Greek King.

'My O?' he lamented. 'It is a sad tale I have to tell. Your daughter whom I took for a wife a short while ago I have brought back today cold and dead.'

'Well now,' says the Greek King, 'that's the finest sight I ever did see! You to be coming today and she along with you even if she is dead. You saved me. I can only be killed by the sword sharpened with the blood of my daughter. Do you know you're the best warrior who ever came to this castle!'

He lifted the trunk and the head of his daughter and carried them to the finest parlour in the castle. 'Maybe we could restore her to life yet. There's a swan comes out of that rock down there every seven years and the blood of that swan has the power to restore the dead to life. She is due to come out again any of these days.'

Away went the King himself and he lay in hiding near the rock and sure he was only a day waiting when out comes the swan and he grabbed her by the feet. He drew her blood and brought a vessel of it up to the castle. He put the head back on the trunk and rubbed the blood on the wound. Anna, his daughter, came to in a couple of seconds and was as hail and hearty as ever she had been. You can't beat a swan's blood for bringing the dead to life! They stayed a while with the Greek King and then went back to Finn MacCool in Ireland.

Finn was lepping out of his skin with joy to see the pair of them again and they went hunting every day but from then on Anna came with them.

This evening they came back and wasn't there an invitation waiting for Finn asking him over to the castle of the Viking King for a big feast. Finn was under geasa* not to refuse any invitation he got so he told Ceadach about it.

'My wife won't give me leave to go with you anyhow for fine well she knows it's a treacherous invitation you've got. There is a well down there where she washes her hands and face and there isn't a request you make at the same well but must be granted. Go down tomorrow morning when she's washing and ask her to let me go with you to the feast on the borders of Norseland.'

'Isn't this the fine place to ask such a request when you know I can't refuse you?' Anna said. 'I know these are the tricks of my husband. I'll have to let him go with you this time but on one condition. When you are returning if he is dead fly a black flag but if he's alive and well fly a white one.'

'Fair enough I'll be bound by that condition,' Finn replied.

They rigged a great ship, and put on board a store of provisions and set sail. It was still dark when they reached the boundaries of Norseland. Ceadach had a good knowledge of Norseland and knew fine well where they'd be preparing the feast. He asked Finn and his warriors to remain on board. He would slip into the castle and find out what was going on.

He stole through the pine trees stealthily and slipped into the castle through a side door. The first one he met was a wizened old man sitting near the fire toasting a tiny oaten-meal scone and he had a very small pot boiling over the fire.

'My O!' says the old fellow, 'I didn't think there was anyone afoot so late at night.'

'Indeed I wouldn't be afoot either but I'm under geasa* not to exercise or do my physical training in the daytime. Isn't it the devil!'

The old fellow put chat on him.

'What,' says Ceadach, 'has you up at this time of night?'

'Well I'll tell you for what,' says the old fellow, 'it's like this. There's a great banquet to be held here in the castle and Finn MacCool and his Fianna are to be the guests. Ceadach son of the King of Tullagh from Ireland is also to be here, you know the playboy who swiped the Greek King's daughter from our Felim?'

'I know, I know,' says Ceadach, 'a wild man too!'

'Oh, the devil out of hell!' declared the old fellow. 'They're to come here and they're all to be slaughtered. I'm posted here these seven years and I can't let the scone burn or the mark of ashes fall on it. Along with that the pot must be kept at the boil. It's a wild handling I can tell you. In all that time I didn't get as much as one wink of sleep. But isn't it worth it to get them all slaughtered, the loudmouths!' says the old fellow.

'Well,' says Ceadach, 'according to the rumours I hear of Finn and the Fianna one of them would swallow that scone in one bite.'

'But you don't understand. The more you eat off this

scone the larger it gets until the table is covered with bread. But you can't let it be burnt with the fire or stained with ashes. The same goes for the pot. As soon as a portion is ladled from it the meat and "kitchen" multiplies so that there's lashings and leavings of food and drink for all.'

'But Finn MacCool and the Fianna are strong, fighting men. How do you propose to destroy them?'

'Well I'll tell you how,' says the old fellow. 'The King's men will be dressed as ladies in silks and satins and each one of them has a dagger. They'll be seated at table alongside Finn and his men. At a given signal each "lady" will stick her dagger in the heart of the man beside her. Not one of the enemy will escape.'

'I see,' says Ceadach. 'Your methods are sudden. You won't be too long polishing them off tomorrow.'

'We won't,' says the old fellow, 'but there's a devil of a sleepiness on me. Would you mind keeping an eye on the scone and the pot until I get a couple of winks?'

'I'll do that and welcome,' says Ceadach, 'but the one thing that worries me is how will I waken you?'

'Oh, don't fret about that. The deepest sleep I was ever in can be broken. All you have to do is give me an almighty kick in the backside and it will waken me.'

The old bucko went to sleep and Ceadach made off with the magic scone and pot as far as the ship. Finn MacCool and his men ate a huge tightener.* Ceadach was back in the castle before daybreak and left the scone before the fire and the pot on the crook over the fire where he had got it. He gave the old boyo a fierce kick in the backside and woke him up saying he'd have to be on his way and get some exercise before daybreak.

He returned to the ship. There was no gathering or community of men going around in those days that hadn't a fool or a clown with them. So Ceadach dressed up as a fool with a suit of green ivy and a large hat of the same plant. When dressed like this no one would recognise him.

The fool went along with the rest to the castle the following day to partake of the feast. The tables were laid out with the finest of food and drink and the ladies were dressed in silk and satin gowns. Finn went ahead of his men although he knew how things had been arranged. He enquired off the Viking King what way were the guests seated at the festive table in his country.

There was a hearty welcome for Finn and his men of course and then the King explained how a host entertained his guests at table. 'We like to get the greatest fun and crack out of our feast,' says he, 'and this can only be done by pairing off the men and the women so that they can nudge and rub shoulders with one another to their heart's content while they are eating.'

'That's not the way we work at all,' says Finn.'We put the men on one side of the table and the women on the other. A man gets a better chance to view a girl he is taking a notion of when she's facing him than if he had to take sideway glances at her. We wouldn't think of mixing them through each other at all over in Ireland. I am asking you to arrange the ladies on one side of the table and the gentlemen on the other side. If you don't do that we won't stay for the banquet at all.'

Finn's dander was up and in order to placate him the King complied with his wishes. Down they sat to the banquet and the ladies still had their daggers ready and Ceadach was waiting for the ructions to begin. His men were ready and so were Finn's and he himself was clowning around the banquet hall, spilling juice on one wall and bowls of soup on another and destroying the lovely dresses the ladies wore. In the end they were all milling around ill-temperedly shoving and pushing. Finally Finn's men turned on the Vikings and beat them badly. Those who didn't escape they put to death.

When the fighting was over and Finn's men were leaving there came a gust of wind and it blew the ivy hat off Ceadach. Felim, the son of the Viking King, was stuck in under the crane-crook and the daylight scared out of him. He recognised Ceadach and demanded the first blow.

'Well, I never promised a man anything that I didn't give,' says my bold Ceadach. 'Strike your blow.'

Felim came forward, drew his sword and cut Ceadach in two. Finn brought the corpse of the dead man with him to the ship and they came back to Ireland victorious and they left few alive in Norseland.

Finn MacCool knew that if he flew the black flag the Greek King's daughter would sink the ship with her magic spells. So he flew the white one. Anna was watching from the battlements of the castle and saw the white flag. She hurried down to the shore to greet them.

She asked Finn if he had Ceadach with him.

'To be sure I have him with me but it's a sad, sorrowful tale I have to tell. He's dead.'

'Well,' she says, 'it was Ceadach saved every man jack of you today for if you had flown the black flag not one of you would have put a foot on the sod of Ireland today!'

She was distracted with grief and had the corpse taken up to be waked in the best room of the castle. She asked Finn to make a wooden box big enough to hold herself and Ceadach and to put it to sea without a sail. Finn complied with her request though he was sick with sorrow to part with Ceadach, the best comrade he ever had. There came a couple of calm days after the box was put on the water and it grieved Finn sorely to see the box floating there on the ocean.

Then came a fierce, windy day and hilt nor hair of the box did Finn ever see again. No one knows how long it was tossed about in windy gales but at last it was washed up under the castle of the Greek King. Anna opened the box to see where they were to discover they were washed up under her father's castle. She went up to the King and told him that Ceadach was dead down on the shore in the box that Finn MacCool made for them back in Ireland.

The King told her that he thought he had as much swan's blood left as would restore Ceadach to life. Down they went to the shore and carried up the remains of poor Ceadach and put them in the parlour. A drop of the swan's blood was sprinkled on the corpse and he rose from the dead with one bound. He was as sound in health and body as he ever had been.

'Boys, oh boys,' says he, 'that was a long sleep I had!'

He stood up and stretched himself. The Greek King declared he would never let him out of his sight again but nothing would do Ceadach but to get away back to Finn MacCool.

The King rigged a mighty ship for him and he and his wife set out again for Ireland. Finn saw the ship coming in to land and came down to find out who was in it. He was so overjoyed when he saw Ceadach alive again that he wet him with tears and dried him with kisses. The last I heard of them they were away with two big sheepskin coats on them to hunt for rabbits on the Blasket Mór off the coast of Kerry.

7

The Naming of Lough Finn

When you are going to Glenties from the twin-towns of Stranorlar and Ballybofey and reach the village of Fintown there is a long, narrow lake on your left hand side known as Lough Finn. However that was not always its name.

There once was an old man living on its southern shore in a one-roomed bothóg* or sod hut. Finn MacCool himself and the Fianna were hunting in that district one day and they took the féargortach.* Now the féargortach is a mighty hunger that comes over any man or woman who threads on 'hungry grass'. This, short wiry growth is found only on the grave of a person who died with hunger during Famine times but when it comes on you you'll either die of hunger within an hour or go clean out of your mind.

Finn sat down and bit his thumb from the skin through to the flesh, then on to the bone and finally through to the marrow. At once the knowledge came to him that it was the dreaded hunger had struck them.

They struggled up to the bothóg* and asked if there was any food about the place.

'Devil a bit I have here that man or beast could eat,' says the old man. 'We're having nettle soup for dinner today but my daughter Finngeal's only after leaving to gather a bundle of them. Did you not meet her going down the lane?'

'Indeed we could have but being almost blind with the hunger we could have passed her by unnoticed.'

'I'll tell you what,' says the old man. 'Feargowan here, my son, knows where there's a wild bull. He'll bring you there and if you can catch him, slaughter him and eat away at him.'

Feargowan brought them away out over the mountain ridge to a grassy valley called Dearrachain and there was the mad bull eating up grass and heather. The snores and snorts of him scared the bravest of the Fenian warriors.

They tried every trick they knew but failed to capture the bull. Maybe it was the hunger weakened them and maybe it was that they weren't as tough as they thought they were, coming up from the Bog of Allen and all.

Feargowan laughed at their feeble efforts. In the heel of the hunt he took a running race and jumped straddle-legged on the bull's back and knocked him cold with a sling stone he had in his waistcoat pocket. The bull went down like a log and he drove a dagger into its heart. They flayed and quartered the animal but it took two of the Fianna to carry a quarter of the great animal. Feargowan got tired looking at them puffing and blowing and trying to carry the beast. He hoisted a quarter on each of his shoulders and tore away up the ridge and down to the bothóg* where his father had kindled a great fire of bog oak outside to roast the animal.

When the meal was over and the beef washed down with gallons of cool, lough water, Finn asked the old man to let his son come with them for seven years to learn the tricks and the trade of war and the kingly game of battle.

'I promise you that when he comes back fully trained there won't be a warrior his equal within the four shores of Ireland nor beyond!' declared Finn. However, it was not Feargowan's good Finn was thinking about. He was very jealous of the mighty Donegal man and this was part of the plan he had made to destroy him.

The old man was not keen on letting his son away with them but in the end he consented. Away they went to Glen Colmcille and Feargowan spent seven years with the warrior band and when his time came to go back to his father he was able to put the 'hobbles' or ceangal na gcúig gcaol* on Goll Mac Morna even Finn didn't like this.

The day before Feargowan was due to leave for home didn't they go off hunting on the other side of Glenties in a place called Mallynamuckie and they came on a wild pig's lair. To make things worse it was a black pig's lair too. The sow and boar were away foraging for food so the Fianna seized the nine bonhams* and killed and roasted eight of them. One of them got away. Oscar was holding him by the tail but he pulled and tugged till the tail broke up near the root and off he went leaving Oscar with the tail still gripped in his hand.

Finn knew the parent pigs would be out for revenge and he was delighted. Poor Feargowan had one weakness and Finn found out what it was. He was under geasa* never to obey an order given to him but to do the opposite. So on the night before his departure when Finn asked him to take any path home except the road of the black pig he knew fine well the jealous old hero was planning his doom.

'Finn, you false-hearted begrudger!' he exclaimed, 'right well you know I must go the way you forbade me to go whether I win or lose.'

Feargowan left the camp. He took four of the best hounds with him, Linchey, Marach, Graffy and Grubach.

When he came to the black big's lair the parents were not at home so he killed the bob-tailed bonham that got away the day before. He hadn't gone far when he looked round and low and behold the black boar was in hot pursuit! He unleashed Linchey but the great boar killed him on the run and sped on. Srathlinchey is the name of that spot still.

Feargowan was filled with fear and foreboding. He slipped Marach. That noble hound fought fiercely and furiously but at length the boar crunched its bones, spat them out and tore on.

'Poor Marach,' he lamented, 'one of my loveliest hounds, I hope the men of Ireland won't forget you.' They didn't.

The spot where he fell is known to this day as Meenamarach.

Feargowan waited until the black brute was level with him. Then he sent Graffy into the fray. Graffy was a tough hound. Hard as the black boar snapped he was not able to break bones. Eventually he seized the hound by the throat and bit through its jugular vein. The great hound bled to death.

On came the black boar, getting madder and madder. Fire was spurting from his nostrils and his snout was turning scrapes in the ground like the coulter of a plough.

Feargowan waited as long as he could. Then he unleashed his best and last hound. Great was the havoc wrought on the black boar by Grubach, the hound that took down a hundred elks in their prime. The boar was bleeding profusely from a throat wound. Its entrails were hanging out and one great leg was cut clean off. Still it fought on and eventually broke the hound's back with a snap of the mighty jaws. The spot where Grubach fell is known to this day as Meenagruby.

Feargowan was well away but strive as he could the black boar was closing on him. He drew his sword and prepared for battle. The boar overtook him at Lough Muck and the battle commenced. They fought through sheughs* and bogholes, through marshes and keeby knowes,* sent showers of black turf flying into the air from clamps and turf-stacks like crows blasted from a rookery until Feargowan found the black boar was getting the upper hand of him. He gave three shouts. His sister, combing her hair outside the cró* or bothóg* on the other shore of the lough heard him and said she to her father: 'That's my brother's voice. He's in great danger and is asking for aid.'

She tied three big stones in her apron and swam across the lough. But when she reached the shore the call seemed to come from the other bank. She swam back and forward many times but the echo continued to mock her. At last she got tired and her long hair got snarled up in her feet and with the weight of the stones she sank to the bottom and was drowned.

The three stones rose to the surface again to form the three islands that are to be seen in this lough still. Feargowan's cries for help got fainter and fainter. In his dying effort he slew the boar but sank down and died on the lough shore, shortly after. The father found them next morning on the lough shore, his loving son, Feargowan and the terrible black boar. Both were dead as dodos. Lough Muck was the name given to the lough nearest to the spot where they fell but Lough Finn was the name given to the long, narrow lough where the beautiful Finngeal drowned when she tried to help her hero brother.

8
The Last of the Fianna

No doubt you have heard many stories of the Fianna — that stalwart band of warriors led by Finn MacCool who policed Ireland and practised chivalry prior to the coming of Saint Patrick. Very little is known of them but what scanty knowledge is left to us was passed on by the last of their band to Saint Patrick.

It was in County Donegal Saint Patrick met him first. The man's name was Oisín and he was a poet. One day when the Fianna were hunting up in Glen a' Smole in the County Wicklow a lovely lady rode by on a prancing white steed.

'Stay!' shouted the poet, 'till I write a poem about you.'

'There's no time to stay,' she told him solemnly, 'but if you leap up here in front of me you can be composing as we go along.'

He did and she never drew rein till they landed in Tir-na-nÓg or the Land of Eternal Youth.

There was a great welcome for him there. Harps were playing low, sweet music, beautiful maidens were combing long black locks or letting the sun gleam on their golden tresses and his head was turned with so much beauty and love. Never a harsh word did he hear or a frowning forehead did he behold. One day when he heard a most magnificent blackbird flute its floweriest tune he was struck with the hollow, homing hunger. He thought of the Blackbird of Derrycairn, the sweetest, winged warbler in the kingdom of Ireland. His heart longed to see Finn and the Fianna just once more and to hear the Three Great Waves of Ireland — Tonn Cliodna, Tonn Ruraidhe and Tonn Tuama — bellow up the three bays again.

He chatted it over with his wife, Niamh an Cinn Óir, or Niamh of the Golden Hair for it was she spirited him away and it was she was the perfect wife too.

'Look Oisín, if I let you go you must promise me not to dismount off the white steed!' said she.

'Cross my heart!' said Oisín and he firmly resolved to keep his promise.

Poor Oisín! sure he hadn't a clue what had happened in Ireland since he left it. Time passed so quickly that he thought he had been in the Land of Eternal Youth only a couple of days! When he arrived in Ireland he found that Finn and the Fianna were long since dead and that few people had ever heard of them. And he realised he was away for hundreds of years.

The people had changed terribly too. The wee diribs* of creatures who called themselves men now were more like ants than the fine, strapping heroes he knew. He galloped through the entire country but could find no trace of his warrior comrades. This day anyhow he was coming up to the top of Ballykerrigan in the county of Donegal when he spied six of these wee buckinbarrows* of men trying to heave a stone on to a cart. They were using wooden skids and were trying to roll the stone up the two planks. He saw at a glance that he was twenty times stronger than the best of them

'You don't deserve the name of men,' he chaffed them. 'Change it to mice. When I was young I could raise that stone in one hand!'

They heaved and puffed away but did not reply.

In a fit of impatience he reined in close to the stone, stooped down, raised the stone in one hand and threw it on to the cart. The noise it made on the cart bed deafened the little fellows and they put their hands to their ears. But the saddle girth broke and he fell to the ground and was immediately stricken with extreme old age.

Saint Patrick had just recovered from his ordeal with the

Leitrim folk. He had gone to their county to raze to the ground Crom Cruaidh and his twelve sub-gods on Magh Sleachta or the Plain of Adoration and the staunch pagans inhabiting those parts took a dim view of excesses against the pagan idols. They first stole his goat and then pursued him to the Drowes River with pitchforks and graips.*

Fortunately the Christian salmon of Tirconnell swam in tightly together and formed a living raft to ferry him across. When he reached the safety of the Donegal bank he stood and shook a saintly fist back at them.

'Leitrim!' he declared, 'I dread you.'

He turned to the Drowes and blessed it. 'Drowes may you never want a salmon either on a summer's day or a winter's night.' To this day there are plenty of salmon in the River Drowes.

So when he came on Oisín at the top of Ballykerrigan he had already set up his Purgatory on Station Island having gathered up the small company of devils he met in Pettigo. He drove them down the brimstone path, back to hell, that at the time led from the cave on the island. You can't go that way any more they tell me. Curious thing, if the people of the Gaeltacht in Donegal want to tell you to go to hell they say: gabh go Pataigo!*

He was now heading for Glen Colmcille to drive the last of the demons and reptiles into the sea. But it was only a half-done job and the good people of Donegal had to wait until their own saint, the Holy Man of Gartan, Saint Colmcille himself arrived to get rid of the boyos with the horns and tails.

'What sea-cat curse or worse sent you to us?' Saint Patrick asked Oisín and it wasn't a very nice thing for a saint to say.

'Hold your horses one minute, a Pháidín!' the old hero advised him, as he straightened up his rickety bones and towered over the saint, 'I was here a good while longer than you.'

Then he told Patrick his story. Right enough Patrick listened to him but he didn't believe half of what he heard. Then Patrick began to tell Oisín about the goodness of God but the old man maintained he was not as good a man as Goll Mac Morna. Patrick laughed him to scorn but it wasn't a bit of good.

'If I saw God and Goll over on yon hillside and that God was to flatten Goll with a blow then I'd give in — God was the best man!' Oisín declared.

'Would you like to see Goll now?' Patrick asked him.

'I certainly would,' said Oisín. 'Wasn't it for that reason I came back to Ireland to see him and all the rest of my people. I thought I was only away for a couple of days. Now they tell me I was gone for hundreds of years. Do you know that?'

'Well, if you saw Goll now and the work he's at you wouldn't think much of him.'

But he might as well have been talking to the wall. Oisín was convinced that Goll was a better man than God and he wouldn't listen to chat about faith and heaven on any ground.

So Saint Patrick brought him to the top of the hill next morning and showed him hell and heaven. Poor Goll was down in hell laying on the devils with a threshing flail and keeping them down in the lowermost pits. Every time he had them beaten into submission the tug of his flail broke.

'Well, I see him all right,' said Oisín, 'but if he had a tug on his flail that wouldn't break he'd slaughter every one of those devils!'

'Well, any request you want now will be granted and welcome,' Patrick told him.

'The request I ask is that the tug of Goll's flail will never break.' And if he had asked that Goll be freed from hell instead that request would have been granted!

Oisín never gave in to baptism until that evening. 'I'll

get baptised myself now,' he told Saint Patrick, 'and I'll go with you.'

'Fair enough,' said Patrick.

Both of them left the hill and went down into the valley and Saint Patrick baptised him. The saint's sight was failing. He always carried his staff or crozier with him and it was tipped with metal. He leant heavily on the staff as he stooped to pour the water over Oisín's head. The point went through Oisín's foot and on into the ground.

When Patrick had finished the ceremony he went to raise the staff but it wouldn't come with him. He looked down and it was only then he saw the pool of blood.

'My O!' he moaned, 'Oisín, why didn't you tell me I was driving my staff through your foot? My eyesight has got so bad I'll have to get glasses.'*

'Sure I thought it was part of the ceremony. In any case I'd rather the staff went through my foot twenty times than to be in Goll's place for all eternity!'

Oisín was now a feeble, old, withered man with no place to go.

'Come with me to my home,' Patrick invited him. 'You can stay there for the remainder of your natural life.'

Oisín went on with him and had an easy time wandering around with little to do and he hadn't a worry in the world.

The saint had made up his mind to write the history of Finn and the Fianna. He wasn't coming much speed at the work until the day he had killed a fatted cow and had it cooking in the pot. Oisín could never get his fill to eat and he was in and out of the kitchen, tearing great lumps of beef off the cooking cow and devouring them.

Patrick was writing away at his history of the Fianna and was not passing much remarks on what was going on. The saint had a servant boy who had a female hound. Oisín heard that the hound had pups. He went out this day to see the pups for he promised the boy he'd take him for one day's hunting before he'd die. He caught one of the pups and threw it on the scraw* roof of the kennel. It slipped down whining and yelping.

'Take it away and drown it. It will never be worth anything,' he told the boy.

He lifted another and threw it up the same way. It slithered down and ran away to hide, the daylights frightened out of it.

Then he grabbed the third and last pup and threw it on the roof. It dug its paws into the scraws* and held on for grim life. 'Keep that pup. It will be a fine hunter when it grows up.' And so it was.

Back went Oisín into the kitchen and he ate away at the beef in the pot. The cook, a young girl who was slimming and had seen more dinner-times than dinners, complained to the saint that the old man would soon have the whole cow eaten. Patrick went in and asked him to stop eating. 'You'll get your share at dinner-time and besides, we'll all be shamed if we have no beef for our guests,' he scolded.

'It's funny to hear you scolding and going on about the wee cow you have in the pot. I saw one blackbird that was seven times bigger than your whole cow! Sure it's only a morsel I'm taking out of the pot compared to the tighteners* I ate in my time.'

Patrick wouldn't believe that he had seen blackbirds seven times bigger than a cow in the old days. He lost his temper and decided that Oisín had told him nothing but lies. So he lifted all he had written and threw it into the back of the fire and the whole history was burned.

All went well until the pup Oisín had chosen was big enough to hunt. Oisín met the servant boy one day and told him the hound was old enough and strong enough to go hunting. The boy agreed but the history and prophecy made by the Fianna were destroyed by this time.

'We'll go hunting today,' said Oisín. 'We'll climb to the top of yon hill. You bring your best gun with you and bring me to the wee rise on the eastern side.'

They climbed the hill and the boy directed the old warrior to the little eastern rise on its top.

'Is there a black rock on this hill?' Oisín asked the boy.

'There is,' he was told.

'Bring me to it,' he ordered.

When they went there Oisín reached in under the rock and drew out a horn. He blew on it.

'Do you see anything coming now?' he asked.

'Not a thing,' the boy told him.

Oisín blew three times on the horn.

'Anything approaching now?' he asked.

'Yes,' the boy said. 'There's a creature coming surely and it is flying. It's the largest creature I ever saw. It has the whole glen covered!'

'I see. That's the blackbird I was telling Saint Patrick about but he wouldn't believe me. Is it near yet?'

'Not so far away!' said the boy and the life was scared out of him.

'Well, you unleash the hound on it!'

When the hound was unleashed after the blackbird he killed it.

'Are you a good shot?' Oisín asked the boy, 'because when the hound comes back if you don't shoot him he'll kill both of us.'

'I'm afraid I wouldn't have the courage to shoot him,' said the boy, 'and things so dangerous as they are.'

'O blast you,' said Oisín, 'it's a pity I ever left the house with you. My eyesight is very poor but show me the hound and I'll tear him to pieces with my bare hands.'

The boy was so frightened that he handed Oisín the gun. As soon as the hound appeared the old hero shot him dead. The hound killed the blackbird and Oisín shot the hound.

'Is that hound dead?' he asked the boy.

'Oh, you've killed him all right,' the boy assured him.

'Maybe now I'll get a bite to eat,' said Oisín, 'something I haven't got for hundreds of years.'

There were no matches in those days but they rubbed two sticks together till they made a flame and started a fire. They cooked one quarter of the bird and Oisín ate his fill. He devoured the whole quarter except the couple of mouthfuls the saint's boy ate.

'What kind of shape am I in now?' he asked the boy.

'Terrible poor shape!' exclaimed the boy. 'You have two red eyes in you like a pig and a belly on you like a poisoned pup. I never saw anything worse looking in my life.'

'I can well believe you. This is the first time I ate my fill for hundreds of years. All that time I spent in the Land of Eternal Youth I never got what you would call a round meal. They expected you to live on love and honey there. Far too sweet a diet. A man needs the savoury things. Look, we must bring the rest of that bird with us to Saint Patrick and we all can eat our fill at least once more.'

The boy wasn't able to lift even a leg of the bird so Oisín rolled it to the edge of a bank and hoisted it on his back, and carried it in to the yard of Saint Patrick's house. The saint came out to see the huge blackbird and said: 'Oisín I thought you were telling lies about this bird. I burned all the old prophecies I had written down from you because I thought you were a liar. I am very sorry indeed. But we can start re-writing them tomorrow.'

'I won't tell you a word about the Fianna to the day I die — when you didn't take care of what you were told already. You regarded me as a liar when I was speaking the truth.'

And that's the reason that the very last story of the Fianna was never told. Saint Patrick destroyed the records.

9

The O'Donnell Prince

Long ago when O'Donnell was chieftain of Tirconnell and had his castle in Donegal Town one of his sons spent all his time hunting, shooting and fishing. Although he was known far and wide as the O'Donnell Prince he couldn't be prevailed upon to practise and perform any of his other princely duties.

When he and his faithful hound left the castle and sped away to roam the woods and mountains of that vast principality no hare, grouse, woodcock or partridge that rose before them was spared. They ventured forth this snowy day and for four long hours neither sight nor sound of the furred or feathered fraternity had been seen or heard.

Then a raven croaked high up on the hip of Barnes Mountain and glided down the frosty air towards the bridle road that led through the Gap. The Prince put the gun to his shoulder. His aim was straight and true. The raven hurtled through the air to fall at his feet mortally wounded.

The red blood of the raven, new-fallen on snow, the white crystals in snow-drifts and the dark plume of the dying bird set his heart on fire. He would only marry a maiden with raven-black hair, skin like the driven snow and cheeks as red as the raven's blood.

But where would he find her? He would hunt no more. Instead he'd sally forth in quest of the most beautiful woman in Ireland and perhaps in the world. He saw her clearly in his mind's eye. Sloe-black hair, snow-white neck with cheeks like the red-blood. Her laughing mouth and pearly teeth; they haunted him in sleeping-time and waking-time.

He roamed the Reeks of Kerry, the Bens of Connemara and the Mamturks. He was seen in the Connor Pass and the Glen of Aherlow. But in all his rakings and undertakings such a fair one was not to be found. In a year's time he abandoned the quest and went back to hunting, a sadder and a wiser man.

One day he was hunting up in Drimarone when he rose a hare. It was a very big hare, indeed maybe a witch-hare. It took off out through the moorland and away through bogholes and marshes with water scooting up over its back but the hound kept close on its heels. They came to the Kilrane river outside Glenties. The hare swam across to freedom but the hound wouldn't stir. The Prince was very annoyed. Never before had his trusty hound refused to cross water but what grieved him most was that the hare got away. Could some evil spell have been wrought against the hound? He sat there for a good while in the saddle pondering his plight and all of a sudden didn't he spy a little boat out on the crest of the river and it was heading towards him. His heart beat faster and faster. The most beautiful maiden he had ever clapped his eyes on; the spitting image of the one he had seen in his dreams, was at the oars!

'Well, O'Donnell Prince, my little page, what's bothering you today?'

The little vixen's teasing me he said to himself, but I'll play it cool.

'To tell the truth and shame the devil,' he told her, 'we have coursed a hare from Barnes Gap to here and then my hound refused to swim across after it! I'll be shamed for ever if the word gets back to Donegal.'

'It won't get back,' she assured him and her tone had changed to a tinkling sweet one like a silver bell. Cupid's dart sank home. He was madly in love with her.

'My dear Prince,' she began, and the arrow twisted in his heart, 'I'll grant you any three requests you wish.'

'Thank you fair one,' he responded in a husky whisper. 'The first request I ask is that if I come this way again there shall be a bridge built over this river. The second request is that I'll never be in any trouble or danger that I cannot escape from and the third request, the most urgent of them all, is that you consent to be my wife.'

'Good man!' said she, 'You'll suffer many hardships before your requests are granted.'

Then she bent on her oars and rowed away towards the western ocean. The Prince was filled with a great longing. When he rose next morning he made up his mind not to eat twice at the one table or sleep two nights in the one bed until he'd find out where the beautiful maiden lived.

Off he went and he was well beyond anywhere he'd be known or recognised at night-fall. There was a sod house or cró* by the roadside so he leaped off the horse and away up to the door he bounded. Beyond the half-door he could make out through the blow-down of smoke from the chimney the figures of an old man and woman huddled close to the smouldering embers for heat. He asked for lodging for the night and was granted it.

'Indeed it's not a great place to spend the night in but I suppose it's better than lying out under the elements,' they told him. He mentioned the errand he was on and praised the beauty of the girl he sought.

'You poor creature!' the old woman exclaimed, 'I suppose it's another case of calf love. I don't know much about this thing they call love. They tell me it has a lot to do with the moon and that no two men go mad in the same way. Our match was a made one and we never were troubled with love and all that codology.'

She lit a stump of a tallow candle and showed him down to his bedroom. Scarcely had he fallen asleep when it started to snow and in no time at all a blizzard began blowing. Snow came in through the scant thatch of the roof and swirled around him in flakey wreaths. When it cleared in the morning he dug himself out of the snow and crawled up to the kitchen. The old man was smoking his pipe and his wife was lilting, 'The Old Petticoat in Mullingar'.

The man of the house enquired if he had a good night's rest.

'God sees to the night's rest I had!' the Prince blurted out. 'It's a miracle I survived that blizzard of snow. Poor Napoleon! No wonder he retreated from Moscow!'

'No blizzard today. It's calm and quiet and not a trace of snow. Now isn't that a curious thing? Whether you take your time or go like the hammers of hell you'll get no further than my brother's house today.'

Away went the Prince and reached the home of the old man's brother by dusk. He asked for lodging and got it. There was an old pair seated at the fireside chatting and laughing and not a bother on them. The Prince told them of his quest.

'Most of the women ever I met were toothless old hags scolding and cursing and tearing out handfuls of hair just because they never got husbands to hug and hold them,' the old man said.

'Yerrah, don't heed that old rickling of bones!' his wife warned the Prince. 'Only I needed a scarecrow to keep the birds of the air away from my stooks of corn he'd never have got a woman for love or charity.'

'If you don't listen to me listen to Goll Mac Morna. He said: "advice of women west or east I'm not taking nor I won't take".'

'And what's this the Cailleach Beara said?' she screeched back at him.

'But come on I'll show you to your bedroom.'

He had scarcely lain down when a hail of black frost arrowed through the roof scraws* and nailed him to the mattress. He could move neither hand or foot. Next day, cold and shivering he crawled out of his icy den to thaw before the kitchen fire.

'You had a good night's sleep last night?' the old man enquired through teeth that held the clay pipe tightly.

'The devil take the frost!' the Prince prayed. 'I nearly got frost-bite down there. I'd have been better sleeping at the North Pole!'

'It's not freezing now,' said the old man. 'Please yourself. Whether you ride hard or leisurely you won't get further than my oldest brother's house this day. I'm thinking he'll be able to give you sound advice. He was ever a terror for high-ranking women.'

The Prince spurred his steed on and kept him at a canter all day. Towards evening he spied a small house built this time of stone and lime with a slate roof and he reined in and dismounted. He found a man and his wife taking their ease by the hearth stone and he was invited to join them. He told them of the fair damsel in the boat and asked if they could put him up for the night.

'You can stay here tonight but we'll have to fix you up in the morning with a faster mode of travelling. You'll need to go further tomorrow than you have gone since you started out.'

He went down to bed. He had just finished one decade of the Rosary when the wind rose. Soon it was blowing a gale and then tore on to a hurricane. It blew the roof off and bore the Prince straight up in the air and spun him down in the centre of the dunghill. As he lay there exhausted another roof off another house came sailing through the air and landed squarely on the tottering old walls. But it was a thatched roof! The Prince roused himself and crawled back inside but he had taken such a buffeting with the wind that sleep was blown completely away.

'You slept well good sir?' the old lady enquired as she made him a bite of breakfast.

'Rest!' exclaimed the Prince. 'Did you not hear the hurricane blowing? Sure the roof was lifted off the house, clean and clear and another one left in its place. If you don't believe me go out and see for yourselves. It's a thatched one is covering you now.'

Both of them hobbled out. As they closed the half-door behind them on the way in, the old man remarked, 'Pride always comes before a fall, Sarah. I told you we never should have had that repair job done. They'll never give us the grant now when they see the thatch! We'll be the talk of the country.'

After breakfast the old man led him to a stable in the wood at the back of the house.

'Can you ride a racer?' he asked

'The faster the better,' O'Donnell told him.

'That's good. You'll need all your riding skill for this lassie. Give her her head. My hound will go with you and he'll lead the way. When you see him leave the road the first time pass no remarks. When he heads for the hedgerow the second time get down and follow him. Keep your eye on the spot where he is scratching. Away you go!'

The Prince sprang to the saddle and rode away. The hound left the road when they had galloped thirty miles or so. O'Donnell rode on. Out came the hound and led him on. Then he veered to the right and began tearing and scratching with his front paws. O'Donnell dismounted and crossed the fence into the trees. He wasn't out of the saddle when the dog was in it and away he sped holding the reins in his mouth. Where the hound had been scratching the earth opened to uncover a flight of steps that led underground. He descended and the earth rolled back and concealed the hidden staircase. He hurried on down and came out in the Underworld. His attention was drawn to a well-kept house standing in its own grounds not so far away. The house was surrounded by a high wall into which was driven a number of iron spikes. With the sole exception of one each bore the head of a man. It was a gruesome sight. The Prince shivered and felt as if someone was walking over his grave.

A man emerged from the house and greeted the Prince. 'Did you come far?' he enquired.

'From Donegal,' the Prince told him, 'have you heard of it?'

'Indeed I have,' the man said, 'you wouldn't be the Gobán Saor?'

'Only his nephew,' O'Donnell lied, for he was beginning to enjoy the game.

'It must have been God sent you so.'

'Or the devil,' O'Donnell laughed.

'Either of them will do me fine. I have a mind to build a grand new house. This one is too old-fashioned. So far any man attempting to build it has failed miserably and paid dearly for the failure. See the spikes on the walls. They bear testimony to their failure. Take the contract and you'll be well rewarded. Fail and your head will decorate that lonely spike.'

'But I have none of the tools of my trade with me,' the Prince protested, 'nor any material.'

'Don't worry. The tools and material will be available in the morning. I'll be down early to mark the site and outline the plans.'

The Prince was up early the next morning and his employer brought him down to the borders of a lake and marked out the site of a house.

'I'm away now,' he said, 'I have other things to attend to. If you haven't the house at the "square" by dusk your head will be on the spike tomorrow morning.'

The Prince was in a quandary. He had never put two stones together in his life let alone build a house and as he stood there thinking of a solution to his problem a small boat drew near and the beautiful maiden was rowing it.

'And what's bothering my dear Prince today besides escaping hares?' she asked.

'My darling, my heart's desire!' he cried out, 'I only thought I had trouble.'

She smiled broadly and spreading a white cloth on the grass that at once was covered with food and drink of the rarest kind, she bade him eat.

'It matters little whether I eat or not,' he said, 'I'm at the end of my tether anyhow.'

'All's not lost that's in peril,' she told him. 'Sit down and compose yourself. You'd never know what we can do.'

He sat down and enjoyed the meal and when he rose to his feet and looked around the house was built to the 'square' and ready for roofing. He turned to the lady and thanked her.

'The house above there is my father's. Every spike in the wall surrounding it bears the head of a suitor who came here seeking my hand in marriage. There is one as you may have noticed still wanting a head. He hopes to have your head on it by tomorrow. I never raised a hand to help any of the others. But you're extra special. I'd go through hell and hot water for you! Away now and cover yourself with mud and let on to be very busy when he comes on his inspection tour. He'll be forced to praise you if rather grudgingly but don't be deceived. Just tell him he's a mean, mangy man who couldn't give you a mouthful to eat before starting you on such a hard day's work.'

She was gone in a flash.

Her father came and examined the work. He could find no fault with it.

'Do you know what I'm going to tell you stranger, I've seen worse tradesmen in my day.'

'A fat lot you care about your tradesmen when you never came next or near me with a morsel of food or a drop to drink!' complained the Prince.

'Come on up with me now,' the old tyrant bade him, 'and you'll get your fill of food and drink.'

He went with him and without the slightest doubt he ate a tightener* that would have done justice to the appetite of the Giolla Deacair.

Next day he was approached again by the lovely lady's father. 'I was thinking there that walls look very bare without a roof. If you can put on the roof before dusk today maybe I wouldn't cut off your head at all. Sure I can get another man's head sometime for that poor spike. It's lonely looking there without a head.'

'I have neither tools nor roofing materials,' the Prince told him.

'We'll soon remedy that,' the old tyrant told him. 'There's more tools and roofing materials up in the store than would roof a hundred houses. The boys will bring them down to you in the course of an hour.'

He was as good as his word. Timber, slates, chisels, saws and nails were left down before nine o'clock.

'Whale away now,' said the girl's father. 'The usual terms. The job done by dusk or your head on a spike.'

The Prince went down to the lough shore hoping that his lovely young damsel would again befriend him. He waited and the boat was rowed in to him.

'And what's the bother today my love?' she asked.

He nearly fell out of his standing. My love? Boy, that was great. Surely he was gaining her affection.

'Much worse than yesterday, a stórín,'* he told her and then it was her turn to blush. 'He wants me to roof the walls that were built yesterday or lose my head.'

'Never mind. Sit down and eat your breakfast. You'd never know what I could do.'

She spread the cloth and the daintiest dishes appeared on it. He ate his fill and then cast a glance towards the house. The roof was on!

Towards evening her father came on his tour of inspection. He could find no fault with the workmanship.

'Hem!' he said. 'I have seen worse tradesmanship in my day!'

'A fat lot you care about your tradesman when you wouldn't offer him a bite to eat or a drop to drink for the run of a whole day!'

'I'm sorry, very sorry. Come with me now and you can eat and drink until you're full.'

Next morning the Prince rose early. Scarcely had he on his clothes when his employer and tormentor arrived.

'I was thinking there that there's not much good in a big barn of a house if it hasn't bedrooms and drawing-rooms, dining-rooms, pantries, bathrooms and kitchens and all of them tastefully decorated. I wonder could you see to those matters today. We'll go down now and I'll show you the way I want the house to be finished.'

Away they went and he outlined in great detail how he wanted the rooms, corridors and stairs constructed.

'If the work is not completed to my satisfaction by sunset tonight your head will decorate that vacant spike tomorrow.'

'Thanks very much,' the Prince told him. 'You're extremely kind,' but sarcasm was lost on the man who did not want to part with his only daughter.

O'Donnell went down to the water-side. The boat arrived and he reached out his hand to the beautiful creature who rowed it. She thanked him, took the proffered hand and stepped ashore. She was lovelier today than on any occasion they had met before.

'Well my noble Prince, any great weight on your mind this morning?'

'I'm as bad if not ten times worse than I was for these last two mornings. He wants rooms, stairways, corridors and toilets and all of them to be decorated before night-fall. It's beyond me. I'm afraid this head of mine is destined for the vacancy on that spike.'

'We'll see about that darling,' she said softly. 'Sit down there and have a good breakfast.'

'It could be my last,' the Prince remarked.

'Keep cool,' she commanded him, 'if you wish to keep your head.'

She spread the cloth. The food and drink were the best

laid before him yet. He ate and ate and when he stood up and looked round he got the surprise of his life. The house was beautifully finished and decorated in a manner that he could not possibly have even dreamt of.

Dusk brought his employer. He went through the rooms and up the stairs. Out he came with a broad smile on his face. 'I can find no fault with any of the work. Mind you I have met worse tradesmen in my day so you have won the hand of my daughter.'

'If I have itself it wasn't without heavy toil. Look at the weals on those hands?' and he stretched out his hands before his employer. He had done some manual labour the night before to make blisters on his hands.

'Had you no cream?' the astonished employer asked him. 'Why didn't you tell me? I'd have sent Maeve in the motorboat to the chemist's to fetch some. Be up early tonight for supper. I'll have some healing herbs for your hands.'

Off he went. He was just out of sight when the little boat and the beautiful maiden glided in to the shore.

'My darling Prince!' she greeted him, 'don't think we are out of the wood yet. When you come tonight he'll admit you have won me for your wife but he'll try to cheat you all the same. There are two other girls in the house and he'll turn all three of us into doves. He'll make us alight on the table and then he'll ask you to pick me out. When we are hopping around I'll ruffle one wing a teeny weeny bit and if you're sharp enough you'll notice it. Then grab me.'

Things went as she predicted. As they sat at supper her father had the three doves brought in and he said to O'Donnell: 'My daughter, whose hand you have won is one of those doves.'

The Prince had the eye of an eagle. He saw a feather on the left wing stir slightly and grabbed the dove. It was his heart's desire all right.

'Were the other doves not as lovely as she?' her father asked.

'No!' said O'Donnell, 'since I was knee-high a fowl merchant always called on my father and he gave nine or ten pence a pound more for the fowl with the fine feathers. This is the one with the finest feathers of all three.'

'I see,' said the father, 'so you've won the hand of my daughter outright.'

They were to be married at some suitable date for themselves and both sets of parents. When night fell and they were ready for bed the lovely lady came to him.

'Better for us not to go to bed here tonight. No sooner will you have fallen asleep than he or some of his men will come and kill you.'

She let down the window and both of them headed for the stable.

'Are you a good horseman?' she enquired.

'As good as ever sat on a horse.'

'You'll need it all before we're safe,' she said. 'Go in there now and select the best steed available.'

In he went and led out a powerful steed that had the strength and swiftness of ten horses. Both of them mounted and away they sped. When they went a couple of miles she asked him to look round.

'Is there anyone after us?'

'We're being hotly pursued,' he told her.

'Put your hand in the horse's ear to see could you find anything to throw behind us.' He did so but found only a little cipín* of a stick.

'There's nothing here only a cipín* of a stick!'

'Very well. Take it out and throw it behind us.'

No sooner had it struck the ground than there sprang up a vast forest that only the birds of the air could penetrate. It halted those in pursuit. They had to go back and get saws and axes to clear a way through the dense wood. This held them back for a good while. The Prince and his true love sped on. When they had ridden another hour or two she asked O'Donnell to look round again.

'Do you see anything dear?' she asked.

'Indeed I do,' he told her 'They're coming again and are not too far behind.'

'Very well. Put your hand in the horse's ear and bring out what you find there.'

He obeyed.

'I only found one drop of water!'

'That's all right. Throw it behind us.'

He did so and a great lough ten times larger than Lough Neagh rose up behind them. The pursuers were forced to stop and build boats and rafts to come after them. This gave the Prince and his sweetheart a good while to move ahead but after another three hour's galloping she asked him to look round again.

'Anything in sight?'

'They're coming again in full cry,' he told her.

'Well, whatever speed is in that horse you'd better take it out of him. I can do no more.'

He spurred the steed savagely and at length they came within sight of the staircase the Prince came down when he arrived in the Underworld. Both of them stood up in the saddle and leaped to safety as the steed sped on. They had only gone five steps when the ground fell away from the base of the stair-way cutting off the approach of their pursuers. On up they went and when they stepped back into Ireland the horse and hound were waiting for them.

They mounted the steed, the hound led the way and very soon they reached the old couple in the house of the big wind.

That old pair were beside themselves with joy to see the Prince again and they were charmed with the beautiful lady he was bringing back to marry. They stayed there that night and slept soundly for there was no big wind or storm of any kind to disturb them. Early next morning they said goodbye and set out for the old man in the house of frost and icicles. They had a good night's rest there and had to throw off the continental quilt it was so warm in bed.

On the third day of their journey back to Donegal they arrived with the old man in the house of snow and blizzards. Again they slept all night for the weather was calm and warm. Next morning they bade the old couple farewell and headed for Donegal Town.

Just a little outside the town, on the Barnes Gap side of Clar, he drew in the reins and they dismounted.

'Better you stay here love, and I'll go on and prepare my parents for the great lady I'm bringing home as my wife,' he told her.

'I'm afraid if I let you away you'll forget all about me,' she lamented.

'I could never forget you after all I went through to win your hand. Didn't I go all the way to the Underworld to find you?'

'Well, I'll tell you this. If you let anything kiss you before you come back to me you'll never return to me.'

Away he went and soon reached home. His parents, relations and friends were overjoyed to see him again and they pressed round and tried to hug and kiss him. However, he struggled hard and succeeded in warding all the girls away who wanted to be the first to embrace him. The dog that used to hunt with him came along and was so delighted to see its old master that it snuggled in to him and licked his mouth. The Prince sat down and he never thought of his sweetheart again.

The lady waited for a while and then she must have guessed what had happened. She travelled on towards Donegal and, as it was getting dark, she climbed a tree to be safely out of sight. There was a spring well at the butt of the tree and not too far away lived a harness-maker. He had a wife and two daughters.

When night fell the women of the house began to do their sprigging or needle-work but round about nine o'clock the mother remembered she had made no porridge for the supper. She went to the wooden pail but it was empty.

'Take this pail Maryanne and fetch me water. I forgot to make the stirabout* at night-fall. There's a grey moonlight outside so there will be no loss on you finding the well.'

The daughter gave a snort and threw her hoops to one side. She lifted the pail and headed away. When she got to the well and looked in didn't she see the reflection of the lovely girl perched above in the tree.

They had no looking-glass in the harness-maker's and this was the first time Maryanne had seen herself (as she thought) since the day her mother brought her to the dressmaker's for a fit-on when she was being confirmed.

She smiled wistfully. 'What a fine girl you have turned out to be, Maryanne,' she told herself, 'but that big lump of a sister of mine wouldn't gratify me to say so. What am I doing cooped up there with a jealous sister, a begrudging mother and a money-grabbing father smelling of cobbler's wax and belly leather when I should be riding in the coach of some English nobleman or Spanish grandee!'

She flung the pail from her and headed away straight to find her fortune.

'What's keeping that Maryanne one at all?' moaned the mother. 'You'd better run down to the well Maggie in case she fell in.'

'No such luck!' declared Maggie, who was a good sprigger* and hated to be disturbed, 'sure there's not as much water in the well as would drown her.'

'You'd never be sure if she fell in headlong,' her mother countered. 'The last thing we want round this house is drownings. They're not lucky you know Maggie.'

'All right! I'll go,' her daughter snapped, and she threw the hoops aside. When she found the empty pail she was puzzled.

'Ha ha!' she exclaimed, 'she's away to close in the ducks!' No one had remembered to close them at nightfall and now they'd be away in the moonlight whuttling* through the guttery field. She'd be splattered with mud going after them!

'Maryanne,' she shouted, but there was no reply. 'She's not in the well and she'll make it home,' she told herself. 'I suppose old slave Maggie will have to draw the water.'

She stooped down and saw the reflection of the beautiful girl's face.

'What a fool I've been! There's no house but should have a looking-glass. What a wonderful looking girl I've grown up to be! But who'll see me in the harness-makers? I'll away now to France or Spain and find a husband equal to my beauty. If I wait until morning they'll talk me out of going.'

She threw down the pail and made off in the pale moonlight.

'Go away Becky and fetch the water yourself. Them girls of ours must be away shinannigging* with boys or some devil. A man sewing a breeching can't live on air. He must have his supper.'

She rose and went to the well and found the empty pail. 'Where had they gone?' she asked herself.

She went down the steps and dipped her pail. Just then the moon came out of a white cloud and shone down on the well water. She saw what she took to be her reflection in the still water.

'I have retained my youth and good looks wonderfully well throughout all my slaving with the stingy old harness-maker and blind-stabbing with my embroidery needle to earn a few mangy shillings. I'll forget about it all and go off to some big city where beautiful women are valued and respected.'

She waited no longer but took off in the moonlight. The harness-maker waited for an hour. Then he went to the well. When he saw the image of a beautiful woman in the well he looked up and saw the Prince's forgotten sweetheart looking down at him.

'What in heaven's name brought a lovely lady like you up a tree?' he asked her in amazement.

'I'm a stranger in these part,' she told him, 'and I thought it would be safer to spend the night up here out of harm's way.'

'Come away with me,' he invited her. 'You'll be much safer and comfortable in my place. It's no castle I know but still it's warm and cosy.'

She slithered down the tree and went with him. In a short while she had cooked him the best supper he had for many a long day. He felt so good that he sewed away at the set of harnesses he was making.

There was a spinning wheel, in the outshot, off the kitchen.

'Have you any lint?' she asked him. 'I love spinning, especially if it's lint.'

'Indeed there's a lock of lint somewhere around the house,' he replied, 'it shouldn't be hard to rustle it up.' He went out to the barn and brought her in the lint and she fell to the spinning.

O'Donnell had some harnesses to be repaired and he sent a servant man out to the harness-maker's to have the work done next morning. Neither hilt nor hair of the leather-man's wife or daughters were anywhere to be seen but there was a lovely young girl sitting there spinning away.

While the harness-maker was viewing the work to be done the servant made bold to chat to the comely maiden.

'Will you come up with me tomorrow night to Biddy O'Barnes for a "treat"?'

In those days a drink was referred to as 'a treat'. 'I will surely, but you must bring me something nice. A gold chain or bracelet would do,' she told him.

'Fair enough,' said the servant. 'I'll be here at seven o'clock.'

He arrived in good time the following night and presented her with an expensive gold chain. She thanked him for the gift and went down to the room to dress.

When they were ready to leave the house she cried out, 'Could you ever wait one moment. I must close in the ducks. There's so many foxes around you know.'

'Don't bother,' he told her. 'I'll put in the ducks.'

It was hard enough to gather up the ducks but when he put them in through the duck cró* door they came out through a hole the fox had made in the scraws* of the roof. At last when he found out what was wrong he had to go off and fetch flags from a limestone quarry to cover the hole in the roof.

When he got back to the house the lady had gone to bed.

'Where's the good in going to Biddy's now?' she shouted down to him from the bedroom. 'The inn would be long closed. You're a nice boy can't close in a flock of ducks!'

He hadn't the heart to ask for the chain back. He went back to Donegal with his two hands as long as each other. When O'Donnell asked about the harness he told him it wouldn't be ready for another day.

'Maybe you'd send the other boy this time,' he pleaded with his master, 'it's a long road and I have a blister on the sole of my left foot.'

However he told the other servant boy about the girl but he warned him that 'if you want to take her out she'll be apt to look for a present and she has a weakness for gold.'

'Fair enough,' said the second servant boy, 'I bet you I have the very thing to please her. When my Aunt Minnie was dying, God rest her, she left me a very expensive gold watch and chain. It being a lady's watch I could never wear it. A jeweller in Ballyshannon once offered me fifty golden sovereigns for it. Do you think it would do the trick? You see I don't want to sell it but it's no good to me.'

'If you give her that I'm sure she'll be well satisfied and you'll have no bother bringing her to Biddy's.'

Away he went to fetch the mended harness and while the harness-maker was putting the final touches on the hames* he spoke to the girl.

'I'll go up to Biddy's with you surely. One gets tired spinning here with only that bleary-eyed old man to talk to.'

Then he presented her with the watch. She was delighted and touched his cheek with a soft, slender hand.

Just as they were about to go out she said she'd have to rake the fire as the harness-maker was away to a card-play in a neighbouring house and would not be back until bed-time.

'Hold your horses dear, sure I'll rake the fire for you,' he volunteered.

However, when he had the coals on one side of the hearth well heaped up in ashes, the coals on the other side had shed their raking and were blazing brightly again. He tried and tried for hours and at length went away for water to sprinkle on the live coals.

'It has taken you so long to rake the fire that Biddy's will be closed. We may wait until another night.'

'Will I take the harness with me?' he asked hoping against hope that she'd say it wasn't ready and that he'd have an excuse to return.

'Take it with you surely,' she told him. 'He put the finishing touch on the breeching this evening and every-thing's ready for you.' The servant picked up the harness with a heavy heart.

Next day he told the Prince about this lovely looking girl the harness-maker had engaged to do his spinning.

'I'll have to go out to see her myself,' said O'Donnell, and he did.

He got into conversation with the girl but couldn't remember ever having seen her before.

'Maybe if you had a house to build you'd recognise me,' she told him. Immediately he remembered the beautiful maiden and the adventures he went through to win her hand. He brought her with him to his father's castle in Donegal and married her. The wedding feast lasted for nine days and nine nights and the last night was better than the first night.

I was at the wedding and I ate and drank and danced so much that I wasn't the better of it for a month.

10
The Derry Merchant's Son

Long ago there lived in Derry city a very big merchant. He supplied all the shops and warehouses from Malin Head in Innishowen to Mizen Head in Cork and from Dalkey in Dublin Bay to the Aran Islands west of the City of the Tribes. He purchased all his stock from the Mayor of London and in time he amassed a great fortune. This day he took a notion he'd cross the sea and visit the Mayor to see how he was getting on. He knew that there would be a hero's welcome waiting for him — for wasn't he the best customer the good Mayor had!

When he landed in London town the Mayor gave him a royal welcome and resolved to give him the 'treat' of his life. The 'treat' consisted of seven days wining and dining in the best hotel to be found and when the time was up, not to be outdone the Derry Merchant ordered another 'treat' to last twice as long as the Lord Mayor's.

When the three weeks were up in walks the postman and leaves a letter for each of the revellers.

The Lord Mayor was first to open his envelope to learn that a daughter had been born to his good wife during his absence. The Derry Merchant followed suit to discover that his wife had given birth to a bouncing boy. Both men were so excited and elated after three weeks drinking and merrymaking that they drew up a betrothal covenant binding their children to marry when they reached the age of twenty-one years.

The document was drafted, signed, sealed and put for safekeeping on a file in the Mayor's safe.

The Derry Merchant came home and, like many a man before him, started to drink. In a few short years he squandered all his wealth and eventually was penniless. His good wife had the presence of mind to put a little money past for 'the rainy day' and so she was able to send her son to a good school.

One day, when both children were around fourteen years of age, the Mayor's daughter was rummaging through the files in her father's safe and came on the romantic document. Being of an amorous disposition she decided to write to the Derry Merchant's son and to invite him over to see her. Until she found the precious parchment neither of them had known of its existence.

The boy consulted his mother who advised him to go and she gave him the money to pay his passage. As soon as they met the die was cast . . . then mutual love together drew them in a fond embrace . . . as the song says and nothing was going to sunder them.

She enquired if he had sufficient education and he told her that he hadn't.

'Very good,' says she, 'here's £100 and when you have that spent come back to me.'

He got lodgings and began to study seriously. When the £100 was spent she came to see him.

'Are you satisfied with your share of learning love?' she asked.

'No dear,' he replied truthfully, 'but I cannot continue to exploit your generosity.'

'And I cannot give you up,' she told him frankly. 'Here's another £100 and when it's spent don't be ashamed or embarrassed to ask for more.'

He thanked her, kissed her cheek and went back to his books.

In the passage of time the £100 was spent and he returned to the Mayor's daughter.

'How goes it now?' she asked. 'Have you your fill of learning?'

'No love,' he answered, 'I'd like to go to a Marine College to master the art of sailing and navigation.'

'All right,' she said, 'if that's what you want,' and she gave him another £100. When the money was spent and they met once more he was proudly waving a Master Mariner's Certificate.

'Good man!' she said and kissed him on the lips. That kiss paid for all his weary hours of study he thought.

She put him in command of seven merchant ships and bade him sail for the East Indies.

'You'll be a wealthy man when you return,' she assured him.

He sailed away on a Monday morning. All went well until he was rounding the Cape of Good Hope — the Suez Canal had not been dug then and all craft bound for the Orient had to go round the Cape. A great hurricane overtook them and his seven ships were wrecked. He barely made it back to London in a small life-boat.

She didn't complain but equipped another fleet of seven merchant ships and put him in command of them. She ordered him to stick to the route he took the first time. He did so and as they reached the Cape once more they encountered a fierce gale and his seven ships sank to the bottom of the sea. Again he just made it back to London in a small life-boat.

However he was forced ashore on the coast of France on his way back, for his craft had sprung a leak and he needed to have repairs done. While in the small port on the French side of the Channel he met a spey-woman* who advised him to have an iron anchor forged in London and to get a priest to bless it. 'When a storm blows up lower the anchor and yourself and your ships will come to no harm.'

He arrived in London and had his anchor forged and blessed. The Mayor's daughter undauntedly put another fleet of merchant-men at his command and he set sail. 'This time,' she reassured him 'you'll return with the treasure.'

As they approached the Cape, Neptune blew up another storm but he lowered his anchor and all seven ships rode it out. Then they sailed into the Indian Ocean and were soon skimming over the crest of the waves towards India.

They sailed into a strong sea current with an irresistible under-tow that drew them right out of the water and into a dense forest that suddenly rose before them. He tried every trick in the trade of navigation to avert this crisis but the ships sped on. As they beached and then wedged themselves among the trees he looked up and there was a large house built among the branches. As he craned his neck to see further a beautiful, golden-haired maiden emerged from the house and down came a ladder.

He went half-way to meet her and enquired how much would she take for befriending and protecting them until morning. 'Three of your ships,' she said, and he was forced to clinch the bargain.

Then she escorted him into the house for a cup of tea. No sooner had he taken the first sip of his tea than he fell fast asleep and never wakened until the next morning.

'You'd best be going about your business,' she told him. 'I have a thousand things to do and have no time to entertain you.'

He got up and went out to his men. Three of his ships had disappeared.

The men heaved and tugged all day but were not able to dislodge even one ship from the vice-like grip of the trees.

At sun-down the golden-haired beauty came to him again and he was forced to barter another three ships for her protection and company.

'You'll be in for your cup of tea this evening. Maybe we could get better acquainted?'

This comment gave him a little hope.

In he went and sat down to the tea. He had made up his mind that willy nilly, he would not fall asleep this evening but as soon as he tasted the tea he was overcome by slumber and the snores of him shook the tree-house.

Next morning he rose to find three more of his ships missing.

So there he was striding up and down the deck of his own ship, deep in despair and not knowing where to turn a hand for help when he spied a tiny, red-haired woman walking towards him on the water. He rubbed his eyes to make sure he wasn't seeing a vision but then the wee woman spoke.

'You silly, simple-minded man!' she exclaimed. 'I'm afraid Goldylocks has completely baffled you. I walked the whole way from Connacht in Ireland to put that huzzy in her place.'

'I hope you'll succeed,' he told her. 'I'm stuck and can neither move east nor west.'

'You'll best her tonight if you listen to me,' the wee woman assured him. 'When you go in tonight leave your unsheathed sword outside the door. As you are sitting down shout that you have left your naked blade outside and that one drop of dew or rain would bring on rust and ruin the weapon. She won't be satisfied to let you go and fetch it yourself but will volunteer to get it herself. When she's away for the sword switch the tea cups and she'll take the tea with the sleeping draught in it. As soon as she falls asleep you'll have her in your power and strike a hard bargain. You should be able to recover most of the sailing ships she has sunk for hundreds of years. Do you see that wood? It's only the main-masts of the ships she has sunk for many many years. They drifted inland and the soil is so fertile they grew up again and sprouted branches. Now here's a tassel. When a storm rises throw it out on the water before you and the winds will settle,' and she handed him the tassel.

'And here's a little skirt. If any girl put it on not even her mother will recognise her. Take them and good luck.'

The wee red-haired woman was gone before he could thank her.

Night came and the Derry Merchant's son went in to bargain with Goldylocks. As they sat down to tea he rose suddenly. 'Gracious goodness,' he cried, 'I left down my sword outside the door. I wouldn't mind but it is unsheathed. If rain or dew fall on the blade it will rust and ruin it for ever!

'Easy my dear,' she crooned, 'Don't get your beard in a blaze. I'll fetch your sword.'

When she left the table he switched the cups. She handed him the sword, sat down and sipped her tea.

She fell into slumber deep. The Derry Merchant's son felt no urge to sleep but kept shaking and waking up Goldylocks and rebuking her for rudeness to a guest.

In the heel of the hunt she cried out: 'if you leave me alone to sleep my fill I'll give you back the ships I sank on you since you first sailed from London.'

'Not a bit of good,' he told her, 'you'll have to do better than that. The joy of your company is worth more than that.'

'All right I'll put three hundred vessels at your command if you leave me alone to sleep my fill!'

'Fair enough!' he declared. 'It's a bargain.'

Next morning when he woke Goldylocks was snoring away but the three hundred ships rode at anchor near the shore and the crews who had been under a spell of sleep beneath the waves were beside themselves with joy. The Derry Merchant's son was the toast of all of them and they proclaimed him as their saviour.

They sailed for London on an ebbing tide and when storms threatened the Merchant's son threw out the tassel and calmed the waves.

As they approached the south coast of England he knew there was a short-cut to London and so why should he sail round by the Thames Estuary? So, placing one of the senior sea captains in charge of the fleet, he had a small boat lowered and rowed ashore. He never once looked back for not only had the tassel the power to quell storms but it could build bridges over streams, rivers and sea inlets and demolish them at the wish of the person who had it in his on her possession.

He headed inland as fast as his feet could carry him and was walking down a narrow road when he was overtaken by a coach. It was owned by a nobleman who was inside, dressed in his best, and he asked his coachman to pull up and give the stranger a lift.

'Where are you going?' the Merchant's son asked him, and he replied that he was journeying to London to wed the Lord Mayor's daughter. The Merchant's son was shaken but he kept his cool. He had been in tighter corners out in the East Indies and rounding the Cape of Good Hope — so why panic?

'Very well,' he said to the nobleman, 'why go the long way round. Take the short-cut, just as the crow flies.'

'But my dear fellow,' began the nobleman, 'that's impossible. Across steams and rivers and sea inlets even?'

'Across all of them and swamps and fens too if such get in our way. Ask your coachman to head for that river and you'll soon see.'

To avoid an argument the nobleman did as requested and as soon as the Merchant's son cast out his tassel a road and bridge appeared over the river. He repeated his performance all the way into the city and arrived there a day before the fleet.

The nobleman was at sixes and sevens. At length he plucked up the courage to ask the Merchant's son his name. He replied as instructed by the wee red-haired woman: 'My name? Well they call me "It's Often Poverty Scatters Good Company".'

'What an unusual name!' declared the astonished nobleman. They drove into London where the nobleman put up at the most expensive hotel. There was much talk and animated conversation in the visitor's lounge and every man was striving to outdo the speaker before him with his tale of personal experience and adventure. When it came to the nobleman's turn he stole the show with a glowing account of the gentleman he had overtaken on his way to London who could build bridges over rivers, streams and sea inlets and demolish them at will.

'And what an unusual name and surname he has: "It's Often Poverty Scatters Good Company" or some such! Have you ever heard the like of it?'

His wife-to-be heard the yarn and got curious.

'You're having us on old chap,' another nobleman declared.

'No way,' his friend told him. 'Any of you who may be interested in checking out my story will find him at the Royal George tonight. He likes quiet little hotels he told me.'

The Lord Mayor's daughter waited for no more. It must be her lover she reckoned. She stole away quietly and made for the Royal George. He was thinking that she'd hear he had arrived and was waiting for a visit. Accordingly when he saw her approach he signalled to her to use the fire escape and to come right up to his room They had much to talk of and it was nearly midnight when he suggested they go back to the nobleman's hotel or there would be a search party out for her.

'I can't return now,' she pleaded. 'If I did my father and his friends would have my life for deserting the nobleman.'

'Let that not worry you,' the Merchant's son told her. 'Here's a little skirt and when you put it on none of your relatives or friends will recognise you.'

She put on the skirt and they went along to the grand hotel.

At the height of the fun as they were dancing a Highland Fling didn't the skirt swirl up and one of her waiting maids recognised her and called out her name. For a short while there was utter confusion but the Mayor's daughter and the Merchant's son slipped out a side door and made their escape.

By this time it was nearly daybreak and someone who saw the shadow of so many masted ships appearing on the Thames spread the rumour that war had been declared on England and that an invasion fleet was approaching. People panicked and fled out of the city.

The nobleman was saddened that his wife-to-be had disappeared and her father was seething with rage.

The Merchant's son and the Mayor's daughter made their way down to the quayside and when the crews who had been held for hundreds of years under geasa* at the bottom of the sea saw their deliverer once more they wept with joy and a great cry of exultation went up from their throats.

The betrothed couple were escorted from ship to ship and at length they were led into a room that was heaped with gold and silver from floor to ceiling.

'This is all yours!' the senior sea-captain told the Merchant's son.

He turned to his betrothed. 'You left the nobleman for me last night!' he declared, 'and now with all my wealth I do thee endow!'

It was a fitting climax to all their trials and tribulations.

The girl's father was drawn towards the quayside by the general commotion. When he learned that the fleet of masted ships included his daughter's long lost vessels sailing home his joy knew no bounds. Now his shipping company would be a match for the king of Spain.

His daughter and the Merchant's son asked to be forgiven for the confusion they had caused that morning and they were. All hands headed away for the Mansion

House and they were married the next day. The wedding feast lasted a year and a day and the last day was better than the first.

In the fullness of time they had twenty-one sons and all of them became sea-captains. You see it was in the blood.

11

The Fisherman's Son

Long, long ago most of the people in this country lived along the sea-shore and were fishermen or harvesters of sea-weed. On the islands they depended entirely on fishing for a livelihood and so the father of our hero in this story could be said to have spent more time on the ocean than on dry land for he was bred and born on the strange and wonderful island of Tory off the Donegal coast.

He was a fine, strong, athletic youth, the most crafty fisherman on the island and by far the best boatman. Is it any wonder then that he broke the hearts of all the winsome womenfolk on the island? Indeed each and every one of them set their caps at him and, signs on it, didn't he marry the comliest of them all; a willow-waisted beauty with long, flowing tresses the colour of beaten bronze and two sapphire eyes that would burn to the core of the coldest and stoniest male heart.

Mutual love had drawn them together and from the day they met until the day death did them part never a frown nor a bitter word came between them They flourished and prospered and had everything they wished for except one vital thing. They were not blessed with a family.

Twenty years passed away and their hopes of having children dwindled. This didn't fuel any friction between them however. They submitted to the will of God, were wise and well-to-do and kept putting by a little money for 'the sore foot'.

The Fisherman toiled on the sea as long as he was able to pull an oar and then he hung up his nets, put the oars away and hauled his boat ashore. For a time they lived contentedly and let the world go by, depending on their savings to keep the fire burning and the pot boiling but times changed, a bad government came to power, and raised rents and taxes and in a very short time their savings were all spent.

There was nothing for it but to go fishing again. He mended his broken nets, painted the boat, caulked* the leaks and put to sea once more. He drifted out on an ebbing tide and was soon clear of the harbour and heading for the open sea. At dusk he cast his nets and hauled them at dawn. There was nothing in them but sea-weed and wind-broken bull reeds.

He weighed anchor and headed back for the harbour. Then he saw her. What a wonderful sight she was! A three-masted sailing ship in full sail. She was approaching him at a very high speed. She had a fair wind and was skimming over the waves.

Then he was struck with terror. It was a ghost ship! The Flying Dutchman or some such! She'd swamp him! He made an act of contrition and doubled his oar-stroke. He might as well have hove-to. In a flash she was an oar's length away, within hailing distance. His eye scanned the deck from stem to stern. Then he saw a girl, as lovely as his wife when she was young, at the helm.

'Did you kill many fish?' she shouted

'Not as much as a sprat,' he told her, 'and we depending on the sea to keep body and soul together and the wolf from the door.'

'My poor fellow. I pity you,' she said. 'Still, I could help you if you're a man who takes advice.'

'I never was above taking advice,' he assured her, 'if it's good advice.'

'You're married?' she asked

'I am.'

'But no family?'

'You're right. We're not blessed.'

'Never too late,' she told him. 'Go home and nine

months from tonight your wife will give birth to a fine young boy. If you bring him to me the night he is born I'll give you the full of the boat of gold.' She grabbed a purse that lay on the deck before her and flung it into his boat. He stooped down to get the purse and when he looked up again she was gone.

He rowed ashore and headed back to the house. When he went in his wife enquired if he had caught many fish. He put his hand in his pocket and threw the purse in her lap.

'That's yours,' he said 'and when you have counted the gold I have more good news for you.'

'The gift is welcome and long life to good news,' she declared. When he told her the good news she laughed incredulously.

'It's too good to be true,' she said.

In the fullness of time she gave birth to a son. The Fisherman took the child in his arms, went down to the shore, put it carefully in his boat and rowed out into the harbour.

The sailing boat and the maiden were waiting for him. She was wearing a mantle decorated with golden thread from the back of her swan-like neck to her neat heels. The fisherman was stricken with her beauty. His old blood quickened and coursed madly through his veins. He had never beheld a woman so blindingly beautiful.

'A hundred thousand welcomes to you!' she exclaimed. 'I see you're a man of your word. You have the infant?'

'I have, even though it breaks my heart to part with him.'

'My good man, I know how it grieves you to part with him, but if you knew my secret there would be no tears in your eyes.'

He handed her the infant and when she had settled it cosily in a cradle on the deck she began piling gold into his boat until the water was lipping the gunnel.

'Are you satisfied now?' she asked.

'I am,' he said, 'if I was not I'd surely need to be a man who couldn't be satisfied.'

He bent down to level out the gold in the boat and when he looked up again she was nowhere to be seen. He rowed back as fast as he could and carried the gold home in dribs and drabs, the way the cat ate the meascán* of butter. It is said that no sooner had the gold come in through the door of the house than the sorrow and loneliness for parting with their child went out through the chimney.

The girl nurtured and nourished the infant well and when he grew to manhood there wasn't a thing connected with sailing or navigation that she hadn't taught him.

One day she asked him to steer the ship while she was having a wink of sleep. He took over at the helm, trimmed the sails, grabbed the jib-sail and away she bounded, ploughing through the waves. When he was satisfied with the course he set her on, he tied the jib-sail and went below.

He found the maiden asleep under a gold mantle. He stooped down and kissed her on the lips. She woke up with a start.

'The geasa* is broken at last,' she said, 'but we shall have to part company. Before I go it's only proper to tell you who I am. I'm the Sea Queen and I've been under a geasa* for nineteen hundred years that could only be broken by a kiss from a man who had never been kissed or had never kissed. I am presenting this ship to you and the other gifts I am giving you are that you never can be drowned or smothered. Maybe we'll meet again but there is no certainty.'

Then she made herself into a shining, white dove, rose into the sky and quickly flew out of sight.

When the Fisherman's son was left by himself he got very lonely for the girl who had cared for him since he was born. He was lost on his own sailing the seven seas and since he could not be drowned he decided to go down to the bottom of the ocean to see how things were there. He anchored the ship and took a leap overboard.

He wasn't that long down on the bottom of the sea until he came on a wolf, a hawk and a wasp that were fighting about a portion of meat they found. None of them could succeed in getting the whole hunk of meat for himself so the Fisherman's son took out his knife and divided the meat into three parts. He gave the largest portion to the wolf, a smaller part to the hawk and a tiny portion to the wasp as he had the smallest appetite. Our three heroes were satisfied with the division and thought that the Fisherman's son should be rewarded for solving their problem.

'I'll give you this gift,' said the wolf, 'that you'll be able to turn yourself into a wolf and that no wolf on the face of the earth will be your equal.'

'The gift I'll give you,' said the hawk, 'is that you can turn yourself into a hawk and that you'll be able to go round the world without once resting.'

'Oh friend of my heart!' sighed the wasp, 'my gift is that when you are in the tightest corner you'll be able to turn yourself into a wasp and hide from all your enemies.'

The Fisherman's son thanked them all and returned to the surface of the ocean. When he saw the wide wastes of water he whispered to himself that he'd like to be a hawk and fly off to see the sights and sceneries of the mainland. The words weren't out of his mouth when he was turned into a hawk and was flying through the air faster than any hawk in the world.

Towards dusk he landed in a wood and in its centre he saw a castle on the top of a cliff and a young maiden sitting inside the window on a golden chair. He flew up on the window-sill and the girl reached out and lifted him into her lap and started stroking him. In the wink of an eye he turned himself into a man again. They recognised each other and were overjoyed to meet so soon again. She sat him down in the golden chair and she sat on his knee. Each of them related to the other the story of the adventures he or she had gone through since their last meeting.

With that they heard an unmerciful guldering* in the depth of the forest. It grew louder and louder. The Fisherman's son enquired what kind of gulpin* could be making such a noise and the Queen of the Sea told him it was the giant who held her captive in the castle since she forsook the regions of the sea and that he was doing his very best to get a promise of marriage from her. She added that as long as there was breath in her bones that was one thing he would never get.

'Is there no way we can stop him?' the Fisherman's son asked.

'I don't know if we can,' she replied. As the giant came lumbering up to the door the Fisherman's son turned himself into a wasp and hid in a crack in the wall plaster.

The Queen of the Sea spoke kindly to the giant and told him she'd marry him in the morning but she feared that a man who had so many enemies might be killed and that she's be left a widow. He laughed at her scornfully.

'I cannot be put to death until that mighty oak out there is felled and consumed in fire,' he roared.

The giant slept soundly that night and when he left to go hunting in the morning the Queen of the Sea cleaned away the mosses and lichens from the trunk of the oak tree and with the help of the Fisherman's son decorated it tastefully. When the giant returned that evening he was delighted.

'I see you are in earnest,' he told the Queen, 'but it is not in that tree my soul abides. There is a wolf in the eastern world with three heads on him and it is in the middle head my spirit lives. There is no wolf on the face of the earth as strong as he, so death cannot come to me until some warrior comes and defeats him.'

'If that's true I'll marry you after a year and a day passes,' she promised him. 'But you must leave me alone until then.'

'Fair enough,' said the giant and he left again.

Early next morning the Fisherman's son turned himself into a hawk and away he flew to the eastern world.

Then he became a man again and set out in search of work. He hadn't gone far when he met a gentleman and they got into conversation. The stranger asked him what was his errand or where was he going and he replied that he was looking for work.

'It was God sent you,' said the gentleman. 'I am looking for a swineherd. If you agree I'll hire you for one month. I have a herd of one hundred swine. Will you take the job?'

'I'm satisfied if you are, ' the Fisherman's son told him.

'Well then, all you have to do is to drive them out daily into the forest and herd them. If there are none missing when the month is up you'll be well rewarded. If you let one of them be killed or go astray you'll lose your head! Is that clear?'

'I'll do my best and I don't think you'll have any cause to scold,' he assured the stranger.

When the bargain was clinched they went into the gentleman's house and had supper. That night the Fisherman's son slept soundly and comfortably in a feather bed. Next morning he had breakfast and drove the swine into the forest. They scattered east and west. It was so dark under the trees in the depth of the forest that you couldn't see to put your finger in your eye. He threw himself down at the butt of a beech but it wasn't long until he heard the roar of a wild animal approaching.

He jumped up and turned himself into a wolf. Then he advanced to meet the other beast. Soon he saw the three-headed wolf approaching and a light in its eyes that would bring back sight to the blind. They closed on each other and the battle went on all day. Towards evening the wolf from the eastern world dashed away blindly, the light of his eyes extinguished and one of his heads torn off.

They resumed battle next day and he lost his second head. On the third day the third head was severed from the body and he fell stone dead in the centre of the forest. The Fisherman's son brought a bottle of the wolf's blood with him, gathered up the swine and went in to his master. He informed him that the wolf wouldn't bother him again, for he had killed him.

'Good man,' his master declared, 'you're the best swineherd I ever had! I'll give you my daughter in marriage and make you heir to my kingdom.'

'I'm sorry I can't accept your offer,' the Fisherman's son told him. 'I'm already engaged to another young woman.'

'I'm glad to see you're a man of your word, but still, any reward you wish you have only to ask it.'

'I'm thankful to you,' the Fisherman's son told him. 'I won't take any reward. All I ask is that if I ever come this way again you will be my good friend.'

The Fisherman's son turned himself into a hawk again and flew back to the giant's fortress. The captive Queen of the Sea was beside herself with joy to see him again and she told him that the day the three-headed wolf of the eastern world lost its first head the giant fell severely ill and that he was at the last gasp now.

The Fisherman's son went in to him and told him he was a famous physician who had come a long way to cure him.

'If you can cure me,' said the giant, 'you'll never know poverty till the day you die.'

He asked the giant where he had the pain and he replied that it was under his left arm near his heart.

The Fisherman's son took out the bottle of blood he had collected from the dying wolf in the eastern world and showed it to the giant and told him it was the medicine that would restore his health. The giant raised his left arm and the Toryman poured some of the wolf's blood on the sore spot. The giant let a mighty roar out of him and gave up the ghost.

The Fisherman's son and the Sea Queen made straight for the main door. They were clear in the nick of time. There was a great rumble of falling stones and masonry and when they looked round the castle was razed to the ground.

They hurried to the harbour where a ship lay at anchor. They set their sails and headed back for home, without delaying until they were back in Ireland. They were wed shortly afterwards and the likes of that marriage feast was never seen before or since.

Glossary

a stórín	— my dear
ar seachrán	— astray
Battering Ram	— used to demolish houses out of which tenants had been evicted
bodach	— a lout or ignorant person
Bonhams	— piglets
bothóg	— a sod hut for human habitation
bruach	— bank of a stream or river
buckinbarrow	— a toadstool
bullaí	— good or stout-hearted
camán	— hurley or hurling stick
caulked	— method of sealing joints with tow rope to prevent leaks
ceangal na gcúig gcaol	— to tie someone hand and foot
ceilí	— to visit and converse with someone
ceaped	— stopped or restrained — do not permit to pass
cipín	— small twig
cogadh	— warring or fighting
cró	— a small roughly built sod hut for ducks or hens
crubach	— an old, crippled cow
crupán	— cramps — applied to cows or bovines only
crupany cow	— a cow smitten with cramps
diribs	— weaklings or very small, dwarfish creatures
drooth	— thirst
evil eye	— a glance that can bring bad luck

Féargortach	— 'hungry grass'. It is said to grow on the graves of hunger victims during the Great Famine of 1847. To walk on it brings on an unnatural hunger
Gabh go Pataigo	— go to Pettigo: a curse
Geasa	— taboo
Grá	— love
graip	— a four-pronged fork
Grawls	— groups
Gríosach	— red embers of a fire
Guldering	— a loud shout or roar
Gulpin	— a very ignorant, uncouth person
Hames	— an article of horse harness
Juking	— ducking, avoiding been seen
Keeby knowes	— mounds covered with a coarse mountain grass
Leif	— like
Meascán	— mixture
Milk the tether	— a witch's spell to steal the butter
Moidered	— confused
Muineogs	— edible berries that grow on mossy mounds in swampy wetlands
Oxter	— armpit
Rí-rá and ruaille-buaille	— rough and tumble, noisy commotion
Scaldie	— wild bird's newly hatched chick
Scraw	— grassy sod spread over roof
Scutched	— slap or beat
Sheugh	— an open, slow-flowing drain. Scotch origin

Shinannigging	— play-acting
Skew	— masonry on top of gable wall
Skirl	— shrill cry
Sliotar	— hurling ball
Spey-woman	— fairy woman
Sprigger	— needle worker or embroiderer
Stirabout	— porridge
Stirk	— two year old cow
Stravaiging	— wandering, strolling around idly
Sums	— a measure equal to the grazing of 5 sheep or 1 cow and her calf (land measure)
Tick	— a few seconds
Tidy	— pregnant animal
Tightener	— a large meal
Trefoil	— group of three-leafed shamrocks
Trig	— tidy or trim
Whuttle	— noise and action made by a duck when it dips its beak in water
Cad chuige nach bhfuil tú ag caint i nGaeilge?	— why are you not speaking in Irish?
Ní raibh Béarla ar bith acu	— they had no English at all
Tá mo chuid Gaeilge caillte agam	— I've lost my Irish
B'éigin domh tréimhse fada a chaitheadh imeasc na nGall. An bhfuil cead agam a dul ar aghaigh i mBéarla?	— I had to spend a long time with the English. Have I permission to go ahead in English?
Tá cead agat cinnte, ach bí gearr	— certainly you have permission, but be short

THE CHILDREN'S BOOK OF IRISH FAIRY TALES
Patricia Dunn

The five exciting stories in this book tell of the mythical, enchanted origins of Irish landmarks when the countryside was peopled with good fairies, wicked witches, gallant heroes and beautiful princesses.

Did you know that there are bright, shimmering lakes in Killarney concealing submerged castles, mountain peaks in Wexford created by magic, a dancing bush in Cork bearing life-saving berries, the remains of a witch in a Kerry field and deer with silver and golden horns around Lough Gartan and Donegal?

These stories tell of extraordinary happenings long, long ago and show that evidence of these exciting events can still be seen today if you only take the time to look carefully.

ENCHANTED IRISH TALES
Patricia Lynch

Enchanted Irish Tales tells of ancient heroes and heroines, fantastic deeds of bravery, magical kingdoms, weird and wonderful animals... This new illustrated edition of classical folktales, retold by Patricia Lynch with all the imagination and warmth for which she is renowned, rekindles the age-old legends of Ireland, as exciting today as they were when first told. The collection includes:

- Conary Mór and the Three Red Riders
- The Long Life of Tuan Mac Carrell
- Finn Mac Cool and the Fianna
- Oisin and The Land of Youth
- The Kingdom of The Dwarfs
- The Dragon Ring of Connla
- Mac Datho's Boar
- Ethne

STRANGE IRISH TALES FOR CHILDREN
Edmund Lenihan

Strange Irish Tales for Children is a collection of four hilarious stories, by seanchaí Edmund Lenihan, which will entertain and amuse children of all ages.

The stories tell of the adventures of the Fianna and about Fionn MacCumhail's journey to Norway in search of a blackbird. There is a fascinating tale about 'The Strange Case of Seán na Súl' whose job was to kidnap people to take them away to a magic island. 'Taoscán MacLiath and the Magic Bees' is a story about the exploits of this very famous druid and about how he packed his spell-books and took himself off to the conference held by the druids of the Seven Lands.

STORIES OF OLD IRELAND FOR CHILDREN
Edmund Lenihan

Long ago in Ireland there were men who used to travel to the four ends of the earth and few travelled farther than Fionn and the men of the Fianna during their many exciting adventures. In 'Stories of Old Ireland for Children' we read about 'Fionn Mac Cumhail and the Feathers of China', 'King Cormac's Fighting Academy', and 'Fionn and the Mermaids'.

THE CHILDREN'S BOOK OF IRISH FOLKTALES
Kevin Danaher

These tales are filled with the mystery and adventure of a land of lonely country roads and isolated farms, humble cottages and lordly castles, rolling fields and tractless bogs. They tell of giants and ghosts, of queer happenings and wondrous deeds, of fairies and witches and of fools and kings.

CULANN AND THE LEPRECHAUNS
Paul Murray

This story is about Culann, son of the famous Irish warrior Cúchulainn. He got his name because as a boy he killed a fierce Irish wolfhound, the hound, or in the Irish language, the Cú, of Culann.

But little is known about his equally brave son Culann. He was called Culann Beag. Beag means small, and our tale begins when he was to have a big birthday party.

Irish Fairy Stories for Children
Edmund Leamy

In these Irish stories we read all about the exciting adventures of Irish children in fairyland. We meet the fairy minstrel, giants, leprechauns, fairy queens, and wonderful talking animals in Tir-na-nÓg.

Irish Folk Stories for Children
T. Crofton Croker

A selection of well-loved tales, including 'The Giant's Stairs', 'The Legend of Bottle-Hill', 'Rent Day' and 'Fior Usga'.

Irish Legends for Children
Lady Gregory

Traditional legends told for children, including 'The Fate of the Children of Lir', 'The Coming of Finn', 'Finn's Household', and 'The Best Man of the Fianna'.